RELIGION UNPLUGGED

RELIGION UNPLUGGED

SPIRITUALITY OR FANATICISM?

MAX L. SWANSON

Cover art: Khepri, the scarab-beetle god of
renewal and resurrection in ancient Egypt.

Library of Congress Control Number: 2007901482
ISBN: Hardcover   978-1-4257-5659-8
                             Softcover   978-1-4257-5630-7

This book was printed in the United States of America.

To order additional copies of this book, contact:
Xlibris Corporation
1-888-795-4274
www.Xlibris.com
Orders@Xlibris.com
38167

CONTENTS

DEDICATION

To my wife, Gudrun, to my children, Eric, Leila, Norman and Tanya, and to my grandchildren, Megan, Liam, Drew, Rachel, Joshua, Justin, Braeden, Trevor, Ian, Patrick and Aiden

FOREWORD

Professor Max Swanson's book is the result of a personal search for religious meaning in the modern world. As such, it reflects a logical, scientific look at the varieties of expressions and beliefs of the major religions today. It is, in this sense, a succinct and factual account of the tenets and practices of such entities. But it is more than that.

The author not only defines these elements, but he also passes judgement upon them, indicating where he finds them lacking, wrong-headed, or even pernicious.

He is even-handed in this exercise, never hesitating to belabor errors coming from his own religious tradition. The book, however, goes beyond just condemnation, as the author offers his opinions on what can, and should be, done to rescue religious ideals from those that make religion into a not so veiled drive for power and control.

Not every reader will agree with the author's opinions, but all cannot help admiring his frank and honest look at a persistent human institution. It is to be hoped that many persons will find new facts along with new opinions from this personal account.

Professor Dwight Hoover
author of *The Red and the Black*.

PREFACE

Like many Westerners of my generation, I was brought up in the Christian traditions, but in a halfhearted way. Although my parents were not churchgoers, they sent me to Sunday school in the local United Church of Canada. It was sort of boring, but I enjoyed some of the lore and myths of Christianity. I can understand how religion attracts the young, idealistic, malleable mind. My older brother was baptized but I was not. Later, when I wanted to get married in a German church, which the parents of my bride demanded, I had to be baptized. When the American baptizing minister asked whether I wished to be absolved of my "original sin," I demurred, saying I didn't believe that a baby was born a sinner. It didn't make sense to me. Fortunately, the minister was a tolerant man, and he asked whether I had ever sinned. When I replied, "Of course, everyone has sinned," he said that was sufficient, so I was lucky. That incident remained with me, as it illustrated clearly the different kinds of ministers and believers—the tolerant, spiritual ones and the dogmatic, fanatic ones.

In my early years, I believed that Christianity was a homey, comforting, and benign influence. I was not aware of the past crimes of religion, such as the Crusades, Inquisition, colonization, residential schools, and sex scandals. It must be difficult for the modern religious person. How can religious transgressions be reconciled with the innate goodness of religious ideals?

I now realize that there is a religious war going on within the minds of modern humans. The war is on two fronts. The first is a struggle between religious and nonreligious people. Nonreligious people think that religious dogma is a fantasy of silly myths. They paint all believers with the brush of fanaticism. They associate religion with those fundamentalists who want to control every aspect of our lives, who oppose stem-cell research, gay relationships, birth control, and worshipping the gods of our choice. In contrast, religious people have a strong sense of spirituality and a purpose in life. They want to help and love others. They are sorry for those who lack faith.

The second war front is between spirituality and fanaticism within each religion. Spiritual people just want to worship God and to obey the primary commandment of most religions, "Do unto others as you would have them do unto you." They believe that the spirit of God dwells in everyone. Fanatics want everyone to conform to their concept of religion. Fundamentalists are fanatics when they want to impose their will on others. If they believe that every newborn baby in the world is a sinner, and that those who are not baptized in the Christian faith will end up in Hell, they are fanatics. If they believe that homosexual people are evil, and not just different because of their genes, they are fanatics.

And so I wanted to write a book about the conflict between spirituality and fanaticism in religion. I believe that religion is innately good; but that it has been corrupted by fanaticism, lust for power, and inflexibility. These three flaws of humans have almost destroyed religion, but it struggles on, led by its basic driving force—spirituality. I believe that religion will never die. The salvation of religion lies with a return to spirituality, and with universal liberal education, improved communication among different religions, and democratization of all religions.

Acknowledgments

I appreciate invaluable advice and encouragement from my wife, Gudrun. Special thanks to Dwight Hoover for reading the manuscript and suggesting additions. Norman Swanson provided the book title, and gave outstanding encouragement and support. Jennie Forster made initial wise recommendations for organization and thrust of the book. Later, she edited the book extensively, making many helpful comments. Eric Swanson and Darren Mollot provided sage advice. The staff at Xlibris have been very supportive and helpful, especially the text editor, Faronah L. Bojos.

INTRODUCTION

*If you would be a real seeker after truth, it is necessary
that at least once in your life you doubt, as far as
possible, all things.*—Rene Descartes

Through the ages, religion has been the obsession of
humans, perhaps their most important activity other than the
basic struggle for survival of the species. Religion has created
more terror, anxiety, torture, and war, but also more solace,
comfort, and moral structure than any other human endeavor.
More time has been spent studying and writing about religion
than any other subject. Countless generations of scholars have
analyzed holy scriptures, and such studies have by no means
diminished in recent times. The present work will attempt to
simplify the treatment of religion by a systematic breakdown
of its components. The emphasis will be to compare the
basic spirituality inherent in all religions with the dogmatic,
literal, and fundamentalist approach, which ultimately leads to
fanaticism—the bane of religion.

Humans have probably been religious ever since they
developed the ability to reason, and learned to fear the unknown,
to realize their mortality and to wonder about the purpose of
life. Prehistoric evidence of religion exists in ancient fertility
sculptures from about thirty thousand years ago, and in the
beautiful cave paintings of southern France from about eighteen
thousand years ago.

Religion has different meanings for diverse cultures and
individuals. In Christianity alone, there are some thirty thousand
different sects or faiths. For some people, religion may mean

---

faith, a sense of community and belonging, or a system of values. Ultimately, the deepest meaning is a sense of spirituality, which transcends individual personality or unique religious doctrines. Opposing this ideal has always been a fanatic belief in the superiority and righteousness of a particular faith. Fanaticism is fed by the lust for power; that is, an overwhelming desire for control over the minds and bodies of fellow humans. Such lust is a basic human flaw, as described in Buddhism. Religious power can take the form of spiritual, emotional, cultural, sexual, personal, and territorial power. Religion has always suffered under the yoke of the eternal struggle between spirituality and the fanatic lust for power.

Religion is primarily based on spirituality, that is, the belief in divine spirits. The spirits can be gods, or simply the divine aspects of natural things such as animals, the sun and stars, or even rocks. In some religions like Shinto and Hinduism, the spirits are pervasive, taking many forms. A faith is called animism when the spirits reside in animals; or naturism when the spirits can exist in any natural thing. In the monotheist religions, Judaism, Christianity, and Islam, the ultimate and omnipotent spirit is called Jehovah (Yahweh), God, and Allah respectively.

Religion also includes faith in a system of doctrines, laws or moral codes, all of which have to be obeyed. This aspect of religion, a result of human organization, already departs from the original notion of spirituality. The introduction of a necessity for faith in these laws and dogmas is the first manifestation of the corruption of religion by men seeking power. In the history of religion, it was men, not women, who were responsible for this development since most religions were conceived and controlled by men (patriarchs). Many different sets of religious laws were developed by different religions. Usually, they included a moral code of conduct, as well as religious rites, including worship and sacrifices to the gods.

Later, more formal religious organization and government developed, giving more power and responsibility to the religious leaders, and creating more potential for corruption. Power corrupts. Just look at politicians. At first, he (or she) is the popularly elected leader who wants to achieve good things. Then, inevitably, power goes to the leader's head, and he becomes more autocratic. Examples abound, such as the Roman leader who later made himself emperor, Julius Caesar, and more recently, popular leaders like Idi Amin of Uganda and Robert Mugabe of Zimbabwe. Thus some nations, such as the USA, restrict the time their leaders may remain in power. Unfortunately, religious leaders usually have lifetime appointments.

The combination of power and religious fervor is a formula for disaster. Many religious leaders use the spiritual aspect of religion to claim that their edicts and wisdom are received directly from the gods. History shows that these leaders are often mistaken in their decisions, usually because they want to retain or extend their power. For example, the Popes of the Roman Catholic Church persecuted certain groups that they thought were a threat to their power, like the Cathars, the Lutherans, and the Anabaptists. Other Popes initiated the disastrous Crusades, and the iniquitous Inquisition, for the same reasons. Could such cruel decisions really come from God?

An individual's conviction that his religion or his sect of a religion is better than any other is a common consequence of a strong religious faith. Faith means belief in something that is not verified, and in fact that often defies logic. Faith is essential for religion. Fanatic religious people often believe that all those having a different faith are evil, and deserve to be destroyed by the will of God. Both secular and religious leaders who wish to exercise their power frequently incite religious fanatics to help them, as occurred for the previously mentioned Crusades, Inquisition, etc., and still occurs for the modern Islamic jihad. Fanatics can best be controlled through the strong intervention of the mainstream believers.

If any logical and humane person considers the many wars, persecutions and atrocities caused by religion, and the weird beliefs and myths of religion, why would he become religious? Perhaps because of the spirituality inherent in everyone, and because of the desire to belong to a moral, supportive group. Much good has been achieved by religions: chiefly, the organization of society and the establishment of moral codes for human behavior. The recognition that religions are made by man, not by God, is the necessary first step for the improvement of the world's religions in the future. The purpose of this book is to consider what is "right" and "wrong" about several aspects of religion. The conclusion is that three great enemies of religion exist and come from within the psyche of man. They are fanaticism, the lust for power, and inflexibility. Religious leaders and the laity can overcome them by promoting more liberal education, more open communication among religions, better democratization of religions, and a return to spirituality.

1

FAITH

Before God we are all equally wise—and equally foolish.
—Albert Einstein

The function of prayer is not to influence God, but rather to change the nature of the one who prays.
—Soren Kierkegaard

We have to live today by what truth we can get today, and be ready tomorrow to call it falsehood.
—William James

1.1 Overview

Faith is the cornerstone of religion, because religions are based on unquestioning belief in the supernatural or divine, and also in the laws that the prophets are supposed to have received from the divine spirits or gods. It is true that some religions, such as Confucianism and Buddhism, are more philosophies than religions since belief in the divine was not originally part of those faiths. However, through history, the followers of those faiths also gradually attributed divine qualities to the founders, Confucius and the Buddha.

Myths form the basis of most religions, both the lore and rites of the religions, and often also their basic doctrines and philosophies.

A myth is a traditional story, apparently having historical basis and serving to explain some phenomenon of nature, or the origin, beliefs, customs or religious rites of man (*Webster's New Universal Unabridged Dictionary, s.v. "myth"*). There are many examples of the adaptation of myth to religion. The Jewish and Christian Great Flood story of Genesis is based on the older Gilgamesh myth of Sumeria. The concept of the virgin birth adopted by Christianity was common in many cultures, including American aboriginal peoples. The Christian dogma of the original sin or "fall from grace" is related to the Eastern mythology of the Separation of Heaven and Earth. Thus, faith in these religious dogmas originated in faith that these ancient myths were true.

The complex relationship between ancient myths and religions has been discussed extensively by Joseph Campbell (1903-1987). He wrote the insightful books *The Hero with a Thousand Faces, The Inner Reaches of Outer Space: Metaphor as Myth and as Religion,* and *The Power of Myth* (with Bill Moyers). His main thesis in the first two books is that common themes run through ancient myths from around the world, and that these themes are incorporated into many of the major religions. For example, the virgin birth, afterlife, Heaven and Hell, the concept of a "hero," and the idea of a "good" god and a malevolent god were universal, age-old concepts that are major components of many religions. He classified many of these myths as metaphors, since they are, in fact, like literary metaphors, e.g., screaming headlines, virgin birth. He noted that many scholarly interpreters of religious texts elevated these myths to the level of primary doctrines or the dogmas of major religions.

Campbell also developed the idea that myths can be defined as other people's religions. His contention is that religion, similarly, can be defined as "misunderstood mythology," since religions are based on the acceptance of myths as hard facts. For example, in Christianity, the virgin birth was elevated from a myth to a historical fact and became a cornerstone of Christianity[1]. For more than four centuries after the birth of Christ, the Church

---

[1]   In his book, *Gospel Truth: The New Image of Jesus Emerging from Science and History, and Why it Matters*, Russell Shorto, discusses the evident

had not determined whether Mary conceived Jesus directly from God, or whether Jesus was born a human and later elevated to a god on his baptism in the river Jordan. There, according to Mark 1:11, "he saw the heavens opened and the Spirit descending upon him like a dove, and a voice came from heaven, 'Thou art my beloved son, and with thee I am well pleased." At the church council held in the famous religious city of Ephesus, Turkey, in 431, it was finally decided that Mary was literally the Theotokos, "mother of God." As often occurs in religious practice, once a major decision such as this is made, it is folly to refute it. Bishop Nestorius of Constantinople opposed this decision and was consequently banished to an Egyptian desert. Those Christian communities of Syria and Asia Minor who agreed with Nestorius were sensible enough to emigrate to Persia, where they established a "Nestorian" Christian church that flourished for centuries in central and East Asia.

In Christianity, the historical fact of Christ's crucifixion has become a myth representing man's redemption from his "original sin." The idea of the original sin or Fall from Grace in the Garden of Eden, on the other hand, is a myth that has been converted into a historical fact. The Fall is just a variant of the age-old idea of the Separation of Heaven and Earth, whereby the spirituality of all physical manifestations is temporarily lost, and man must again find his spiritual connection with all parts of the universe. Campbell notes that the blending of history and myth in the doctrine of salvation through the death of Christ has "such compelling fascination that both the psychological and the metaphysical connotations of the metaphoric symbols have been all but lost . . ." As Campbell asks, "What in the name of Reason or Truth is a modern mind to make of such evident nonsense?" (*The Inner Reaches of Outer Space: Metaphor as Myth and as Religion*)

---

myth of the virgin birth. In the first Gospel, Mark, written about thirty-five years after Jesus's death, and in Paul's letters, written about fifteen years after Jesus's death, no mention of the virgin birth was given. It was only revealed in the later Gospel of Matthew, presumably because Christians wanted to convert Greeks, who were used to the virgin birth myth of their pagan gods.

Faith in divine spirits, and in the prophets who were supposedly given direct instructions from the gods, has led to a diverse collection of religions. Christianity is the largest religion, dominating in Europe and the Americas. It is challenged by Islam, the other major confrontational, proselytizing religion, which dominates in Indonesia, the Middle East, and parts of Africa and Asia. Regional religions such as Hinduism, Shinto, and to some extent Buddhism, dominate in some populous Far Eastern nations such as India and Japan. In China, previously a center for "philosophical" faiths such as Buddhism and Confucianism, many years under Communist rule almost eliminated religion. However, since the economic reforms of the 1980s, China has permitted some state-controlled religions, including Buddhism, Taoism, Islam, Catholicism, and Protestantism. In addition, many illegal sects have arisen, especially in rural areas. Polls indicate that 10-30 percent of Chinese now practice some form of religion. In Russia, which was the world center of the Eastern Orthodox form of Christianity before its period under Communism from 1917 to 1990, religious practice seems to be rekindled. In modern, developed nations, followers of religion are in decline, especially in Europe. In England, only about 15 percent of the population attends church. In the USA, however, religion is still strong as 75 percent of the population claims to be religious. This is a startling difference. It may indicate a lack of critical thinking in the USA. Or, it may be a reaction to the overindulgence of the senses, and the apparent decline in morality of the modern generation. Perhaps it is the beginning of a new cycle of religious fervor, an attempt to find a meaningful and redemptive life.

Because religion is so widespread, it appears that it is an essential part of the human psyche. Religion involves more than just believing in divine spirits to explain the unknown and prophets to supply a moral code. Man needs to have faith in his fellow men and to live in a social group that provides physical and moral support. In times of need, the help of family, community, or state may be lacking, or may not be enough. A supporting group like a religious sect, which provides a sense of belonging and security, is important.

All religions have evolved through history, sometimes beneficially, and sometimes not. In the past, the transgressions of religions, especially Christianity, were appalling. They were caused by lust for power and by fanatical intolerance of other religions and "heretical" sects. Some of the Christian transgressions were the Crusades, the annihilation of the Cathars and the Anabaptists, the Inquisition, the persecution of the Protestants and Jews, and the colonial atrocities. Christian faiths now are much more tolerant than they were in their shockingly violent past. Now, almost any unusual Christian sect is tolerated in modern secular nations such as the USA and the European States (see Chapter 4). Some of these are Scientology, Children of God, and fringe sects of the Mormon Church that practice polygamy. Other religious groups, such as the Unification Church of Reverend Sun Myung Moon and Hare Krishna, a Hindu sect, are also tolerated. Some Christian Churches even accept homosexual relationships, although this is still a very controversial topic. In many nations, especially secular ones, religious freedom is a legal right.

The faith of Islam has been largely retrograde in adapting to modern times, especially in western Asia and Africa, although it experienced some early developments into reformed sects. In much of the history of Islam, followers of Judaism and Christianity were tolerated and even respected because they were considered to be "people of the Book," meaning they followed the Judeo-Christian Old Testament. However, more recently, partly because of the interference of Western powers in the oil-rich nations of the Middle East, and partly because of the Israel-Palestinian conflict, Islam has become more violently anti-Christian. In addition, while the role of women in religion and society has advanced considerably in the Christian faiths, it has actually regressed in many Islamic societies. In some fundamentalist religious states such as Iran, Saudi Arabia, and the (former) Taliban state of Afghanistan, women's rights have been severely curtailed. In some African Muslim regions, the sexual mutilation of women is commonly practiced.

In religious people, faith in their own religion was often so strong that they would die rather than renounce their religion. The result was many martyrs in the long and stormy history of religion. Legends tell of Christians being thrown to the lions in the ancient coliseum of Rome. Many other Christian martyrs were burned at the stake by the Inquisition after refusing to denounce their faith.

1.2 The Age of Reason

The Age of Faith, so brilliantly described in the book of that title by Will Durant, gave way to the Ages of Reason and Enlightenment in the seventeenth and eighteenth centuries. The advent of the scientific method, whereby so-called facts had to pass the test of empirical verification before being accepted, meant that the ancient doctrines and dogmas of religion were severely challenged. In the time of Galileo and Copernicus, science had already demolished the religious idea that the Earth was the center of the universe. Then came the geologists and paleontologists, who showed that the Earth was very old and had been populated by dinosaurs millions of years ago. Then Darwin developed his revolutionary theory that man evolved from apes over a period of millions of years. These well established theories[2] are clearly inconsistent with the biblical doctrine that God created man and all the creatures of the earth only about six thousand years ago. Incredibly, even today, some school systems, especially in the USA, question the Darwinian theory and require that the "theory of creation" or "Intelligent Design" also be taught. The idea that God created the universe, although fundamentally not questionable (only the date of creation and the idea that Man was created in God's image can be questioned), is not a theory. It is a statement of faith.

---

[2]   Remember that scientific ideas and theories are only that, and not facts. They can be considered to be facts when they are verified by an overwhelming body of evidence. But theories are made to be broken. For example, the Newtonian theory of gravity, although still true for man's macro-world, has been superseded by Einstein's theory of relativity, which applies in a large scale of time and space with which people are not familiar. A theory is only as good as the validity of its predictions.

The difficulty with trying to understand the universe via faith rather than science is that religion and religious doctrines were invented by humans in the belief that particular prophets had received their inspirations directly from God or the gods. It is certainly known that man is fallible, and therefore the doctrines of religion are subject to human error. Moreover, even if the prophets did receive divine inspiration, their knowledge and writings were often passed along by oral history through several generations before they were written down. And those that wrote down the divine words had their own concepts of what the world was about, and therefore may very well have added their own ideas[3]. Furthermore, there have been many errors of translation in these religious documents. In addition, as civilization progressed, concepts about the universe and about man changed. With increased knowledge, man's perception of his place in the universe evolves. It follows that the doctrines of religion, as related to the physical world, were probably erroneous, and also have to be modified in light of modern knowledge.

It is self-evident that faith has its place in every human life. Knowledge based on scientific evidence also has its place. The mistake that religious authorities make is to confuse faith with fact. By definition, faith is belief in unverified and often unverifiable things. Many scientists, such as Albert Einstein, were religious people. However, even Einstein was led astray by his faith when he made the famous statement that "God does not play dice with the universe." By this, he expressed doubt in the uncertainty principle, which states that no one can precisely establish both the position and momentum of a particle. This principle is a fundamental part of the quantum theory of matter, on which man's knowledge of the structure of matter is based. However, there will always remain many mysteries of the universe that defy a scientific explanation. For example, if the universe started with a big bang, what preceded the big bang?

---

[3]   For example, it is now believed that the authors of the Gospels Matthew and Mark had a somewhat distorted view of the involvement of the Pharisees in the death of Jesus because of the political and religious pressures of their time.

Was there a series of big bangs? What created the matter that caused the big bang? How can there even be a universe?

Faith versus science should not produce a conflict. The conflict arises when religious leaders extend their area of expertise, which is faith based, to an area in which they have no expertise. The same applies to scientists.

1.3 The Purpose of Faith

Faith in God or gods, and faith in the moral doctrines of religion, are important. Faith in God or divine spirits enhances the idea that humans have a purpose in life and gives believers a feeling of peace and acceptance. On the negative side, the acceptance of injustices that can be corrected or diseases that can be cured as the "will of God" is a defeatist attitude. On the positive side, especially in the past, when social and political systems were more rigid, acceptance of unpleasant things as the "will of God" gave man peace. Faith is beneficial in times of bereavement. When a dear friend or relative dies, faith that he has entered a better life in the hereafter, that he has earned his place in heaven, is comforting. It enables a person to accept the inevitability of death more calmly. Faith in the innate goodness of man, in the face of many calamities, is also reassuring and is beneficial for the future of mankind. Optimism and hope are powerful elixirs for mental health.

Faith in the moral codes of religions has been a strong force for order in society. The Ten Commandments of Christianity, Judaism and Islam have helped to stabilize society. In fact, it is well to reexamine these commandments today. Although some of them reflect the taboos and ethics of the time when they were written, they still are largely valid (see Chapter 6. Dogma). Eastern religious tenets were also beneficial: the Hindu dictum "from good must come good, and from evil, evil;" the Confucian code of ethics and its message "to love others;" and the Buddhist's Eightfold Path to **Nirvana** and its Ten Perfections (giving, duty, renunciation, insight, courage, patience, truth, resolution, loving kindness, and serenity) provided firm foundations for stability and prosperity in much of Asia for millennia.

2

SPIRITUALITY

The spirit of God dwells in you.—Saint Paul

God is closer to man than his own neck vein.—The Koran

Every person is "imbued with a latent divinity."—Carl Jung

2.1 Introduction

The belief in divine spirits or gods has always been a central concept in religion. It is commonly accepted that, ever since humans became puzzled and fearful about the unknown forces surrounding them, they sought to explain these forces in terms of the supernatural. Some of the earliest terrors they experienced must have been thunder, lightning, and storm. It was natural to attribute the loud sounds of thunder accompanying violent storms to the voice of an angry god. Similarly, primitive man associated divine powers or spirits with the large predators that preyed on them.

Perhaps the earliest evidence of spirituality is given by a Neanderthal antler carving discovered at a site in southern France. It is dated at about 30,000 BCE (Before the Common Era, or Before Christ), via radiocarbon analysis. It represents a pregnant woman, with mysterious carvings on her chest. Such a figure was probably worshiped as a spirit representing fertility. Many such carvings have been found, but this one is the earliest.

The famous cave paintings at Lascaux, France, are another early artistic expression of spirituality. This marvelous art, dating from about 16,000 BCE, was discovered only in 1940. The paintings depict animals of that time, including bulls, deer, bison and wooly rhinoceros. The astounding artistry of these paintings clearly shows a reverence for the animals. Historians and anthropologists believe that these ancient paintings were a form of worship. These art galleries have been described by Michael Jordan, author of *Gods of the Earth*, as "mankind's earliest cathedrals." He believes that these animals were worshiped for their power, and also for their life-giving sustenance, since ancient man survived by hunting the animals that he worshiped.

Every religion has a spiritual aspect. The central spiritual concept of many religions is the existence of the divine in all humans. In the case of the philosophical religions, like Buddhism, the spirituality is in the form of meditation. Spirituality is an essential part of the mind of man. It transcends the earthly and mundane aspects of life, takes man out of himself, and makes him humble. It gives a feeling that there is more meaning to life than the everyday effort to survive and to coexist with fellow humans. Humans are born, struggle to make a decent life, and then are doomed to die. Is there anything more? Spirituality gives the answer. A person who believes that the spirit of God exists within everyone cannot feel superior to those of different faiths. He becomes humble.

The ennobling and emancipating aspects of spirituality have often been damaged by religious leaders who seek to utilize spirituality to advance their personal or institutional power. Such leaders declare that their form of spirituality is so superior that it must be forced on everyone. It is the only mystical way that is "right." All other ideas of spirituality are wrong, and should give way to their superior one. The result is the institutionalizing of spirituality, which is contrary to its basic nature, one person's communion with the spiritual world. The control of individual spirituality within an organizational framework provides more cohesiveness and therefore more power to the religious leaders. One example of the dogmatization of spirituality is the somewhat bizarre Christian concept of the Holy Trinity, which was presumably adopted because the average convert could not be expected to understand the concept of an unknowable, all-encompassing God. Another example is the forcing of Christian spiritual concepts on indigenous peoples during periods of colonization. The misguided use of spirituality for the achievement of individual or collective power is the root of enormous problems, and forms a basic dilemma for religion (Chapter 5).

Another negative aspect of man's attempts to manipulate spirituality is the introduction of excessive ritual. Some ritual such as prayer is beneficial because it provides a restful time of quiet contemplation and meditation. However, it seems that from the early days of religion, the spiritual leaders or shamans, in order to obtain more power for themselves, introduced many secret rituals and sacrifices that were supposed to be necessary to communicate with the spirits, and to please them. In many cases, these rituals became so complicated and expensive that they oppressed the common man, and even destroyed the lives of some people (see Ch. 6).

2.2 Afterlife

2.2.1 Overview

The concepts of life after death, and the Judgment Day—when all eternal souls will be rewarded or punished by God—have been important spiritual components of most religions for all of history. There is even prehistorical evidence for belief in the afterlife. Neanderthals left flowers and grain at their grave sites. (See *Life After Death: A History of the Afterlife in the Religions of the West*, by Alan Segal). Our knowledge of the marvelous and long-lasting ancient Egyptian civilization is steeped in their magnificent tombs and temples, erected because of their idea that life would continue after death. Their science of mummification was so advanced that perfect mummies are still being found. The majority of people still believe in the afterlife. As Alan Segal says, "[A]fterlife notions are mirrors of our cultural and social needs, available to development and manipulation," and "[T]he afterlife is another way to express the same transcendent, non-confirmable issue of God. The afterlife is particularly important to religions that organize themselves as missionary religions."

The idea that the soul lives forever probably arises from man's fear of death. Humans have always resisted the inevitability of death. The search for the fountain of youth has created many fables, health elixirs, charlatans and disappointments. Most religions have assumed a role in this subject by developing concepts of the eternal soul, which leads to a strong conviction that there is a life after death. The belief in the oneness of God, which also means that God is present in all humans, implies that the spirit or soul of man is separate from the body, and is eternal. Consequently, religions usually consider that the afterlife is a spiritual one, in which the soul ascends to Heaven, or descends to Hell. Some religions also believe in the reincarnation of the physical body.

Religions use the concept of an afterlife to promote their views and their power. They accomplish that by the notion that a person will be judged by God or the gods, either on his death or on a final "Judgment Day," and, in the hereafter, his soul will be rewarded or punished. Therefore, a person must obey particular religious laws or be punished in the afterlife. Usually, in religious dogma, a good life is rewarded in Heaven and a bad life is punished in Hell. Various versions of the pleasures of Heaven and the fires of Hell have been described in religious texts.

Ancient Egyptians believed that a person was composed of the body, the soul, and the spirit. The body was the vessel in which the soul and spirit resided. The soul resided in the heart, and the spirit resided in the brain. The soul was immortal; when the body died, the soul remained for eternity. For this reason, the Egyptians thought that the preparation of burial tombs was extremely important. An enormous amount of effort was expended in mummification and burial of important people. The spirit was considered to be man's conscience. If the spirit was pure and good, the soul would be transferred to a place of contentment and honor, the later Heaven of most religions.

In Hinduism and Buddhism, good deeds lead to a physical reincarnation in a higher status or caste. In the monotheist religions, Judaism, Christianity and Islam, a good life is rewarded by ascent to Heaven. An evil life leads to the soul descending to the eternal fires of Hell. In Christianity, Heaven is a somewhat nebulous place of contentment rather than great joy. In Islam, there seem to be some earthly joys in Heaven, such as beautiful gardens with fountains, and serving girls.

A nonreligious view of the afterlife is that it is equivalent to the lasting effects of a person's interactions with his fellow humans. If the soul is considered to be the essence of human thought and conscience, then it follows that a part of each person's soul is shared by all persons that he has influenced through his life. This is especially true of his close friends and his children. A part of him or her is transmitted to those dear to him. In turn, this part is transmitted further by his friends and children, forever.

Another modern view of immortality is that it is the transmission of a person's individual, unique human genome to his descendants. The powerful urge to reproduce is not only a basic human attribute, but is also driven by the desire to propagate personal genes. Throughout history, the importance of a male heir predominates. Although the existence of genes was only recently discovered, this urge to propagate a person's unique human traits through his offspring is eternal. Depending on the definition of the soul, it can also be considered that the inheritance of a person's genes implies that an important component of his soul is transmitted forever.

2.2.2 Afterlife in Hinduism and Buddhism

The Hindu religion has been practiced by a large fraction of the population of India for millennia. It has no known founder. The word Hindu is derived from the Sanskrit word **sindhu**, meaning, river, or, more specifically, the Indus River. The present form of Hinduism originated about 1500 BCE, when Indo-Aryan tribes invaded the Indus Valley. Many of the customs of the indigenous tribes, such as phallic worship, bathing in temple tanks, and the practices of **yoga**, may have been incorporated into the Hindu religion of the invaders, which developed from their Vedic religion. Hinduism presently has about one billion adherents. It is not a proselytizing religion, but has many emigrant Indian believers throughout the world.

Hindus believe that there is one Universal Spirit or Eternal Essence in the universe, called **Brahman**, meaning World-Soul. Brahman is also called the **Trimutri**, Triad, or three-in-one God. It is interesting to speculate whether the Christian idea of the Holy Trinity arises from this concept. The three gods encompassing Brahman are **Brahma**, the creator, **Vishnu**, the preserver, and **Shiva**, the destroyer, who is also, interestingly, the god of song, healing, and creative energy. These three gods are part of the same Divine Unity, Brahman, who neither loves nor hates, rewards or punishes. Thus, one can classify Hinduism as more of a naturistic religion than Judaism, Christianity and Islam, which believe in a more personified God, in the image of humans. Hindus consider that Buddhists, Jains and Sikhs follow a type of reformed Hinduism. They also believe that other major religious prophets, such as Christ, Muhammad and the Buddha, are **avatars**, or holy spirits born in human form.

In the Hindu creed, the world is thought to be part of endless cycles in time, called the Days of Brahman, each "day" lasting about 4.5 million years. At the end of each cycle, Shiva destroys the old world, and Brahma creates a new one. Vishnu appears in different human forms to preserve the world and to guide and enlighten mankind.

In common with other religions, the soul of man is considered to be separate from the body, or "garment of the soul." The soul endures forever, but the body is discarded when it becomes worn out. The body is ruled by passion and desire, whereas the soul is ruled by serenity, peace and truth. In the **Bhagavad Gita**, (the Lord's song) peace and tranquility "come to him who deals with objects of the senses, not loving and not hating, making them serve his free soul, which remains serenely lord." **Yogis** are religious men who practice Yoga, a form of disciplined control of the body and mind, which is supposed to lead to Nirvana. Yoga has been popularized in the Western world, under instruction of **gurus** (teachers) imported from India.

Hindus believe in the Law of Action, called **Karma**, which dictates that "From good must come good, and from evil, evil."

As a result of good deeds, the soul of a believer is reincarnated in a higher form, and as a result of bad deeds it is reborn as an inferior being, perhaps in a lower caste or as an animal or insect[4]. The ultimate goal of Hindus is to achieve **Nirvana** (comparable to the Christian Heaven), in which the soul is joined with the World-Soul, and is separated from the body forever. This state frees individual souls from the endless cycle of reincarnation. In Hinduism and Buddhism, there is no final collective Judgment Day for humans.

Buddhism began as a reform movement of Hinduism. It originated in India near 527 BCE with the teachings of Siddhartha Gautama, the future **Buddha**. He did not believe in speculation about an eternal soul. Buddhism was basically a philosophy rather than a religion. The two main forms of Buddhism stress wisdom and compassion. Later, Buddhism did develop a hierarchy similar to that of other religions, and the Buddha was worshiped as a God, which was contrary to his teachings. Buddhism retains the concepts of **Karma** and an eternal consciousness (if not soul) that is continuously reborn on the Wheel of Life, in the form of a human rebirth or a residence in various Heavens and Hells. A person can finally overcome the endless cycle of reincarnation by following the Eightfold Path, and thereby achieve Nirvana.

2.2.3 Judeo-Christian-Muslim Concepts of the Afterlife

Many concepts of Judaism, Christianity and Islam, including ideas about the afterlife, stem from Zoroastrianism, which

---

[4]   The caste system, by which there are different classes of people, depending on their professions, and dictated by their family histories, is unique to Hinduism. Although by civil law in India, this system is now illegal, it is still practiced. The caste system originated from the Hindu myth that Brahma created the first man called Manu, and that the best and holiest people, Brahmans, came out of Manu's head. Brahma also created the lower castes, Kshatriyas (warriors), Vaisyas (craftsmen) and Sudras (the rest). The different castes developed into many subcastes, the lowest of all being the "untouchables." The original idea of caste has been corrupted to condone rampant discrimination.

may be the oldest monotheist religion that is practiced today. Historians believe that it arose from an old Aryan religion, based on the sacred Vedas, which also form the basis of Hinduism. The founder was Zoroaster (Latin for the Persian name Zarathustra), who was born in Persia (now Iran) between 1600 and 2000 BCE. It is an ethical religion. The central belief is that salvation results from following the path of **Asha**, "good thoughts, good words, good deeds." God rewards a good life in the hereafter and punishes a bad life. However, in contrast to modern religions, on a final Judgment Day, both good and evil human souls are reunited with God, the "Eternal Light."

In early Judaism, life after death existed in a somber underworld. Later, the religion introduced concepts of reward for a good life and punishment for an evil life. When the Messiah returns, and creates the Kingdom of God on Judgment Day, the consequences of having led a good or bad life will occur. In Islam also, the idea of a Judgment Day was incorporated. After death, the person is asked who is your God, who is His Prophet, and what is your faith. If he answers Allah, Muhammad and Islam, he is rewarded by eternal happiness, but if he does not, the fires of Hell await him. Similarly, in Christianity, passage to Heaven requires faith in Jesus Christ. Belief in a different God or prophet than the one accepted by a particular monotheist religion is disastrous for the afterlife. Even today, many persons of faith believe this cruel concept. Why would God punish those of a different faith, even if they believed in the one God, and lived a good life?

Jesus preached that the "Kingdom of God" was soon to come, meaning that the prophesied apocalyptic doomsday or "end of the age" was imminent, when all good and righteous men would go to Heaven, and all evil ones would suffer in Hell. This was a common belief among many Jews, who were suffering under the hands of the oppressing Romans. Jesus exhorted all to mend their ways, and become better, more humble and more loving. Besides advocating the usual high moral standards of Judaism, he preached that love of one's fellow man was all-important. Jesus taught not only that God must be loved above all by every person, but that God in turn loved all mankind. This personal relationship between God and man is a strong aspect of Christianity. This is no impersonal, mysterious Spirit of the Universe, but a warm, friendly God.

Salvation: Almost all Christians agree that everyone has eternal life, either in Heaven or in Hell. Unfortunately, for most people, this life will be one of endless torture in Hell without any hope of reprieve because of human sins. Only a small minority who have achieved salvation before death will live forever in heaven. Salvation involves the forgiveness by God of a person's sins. The person repents for her/his sins, trusts Jesus as Lord and Savior, and becomes reconciled with God. God makes the person into a "new creation." Some Christian sects believe that a person is saved by faith alone; others believe that both good works and faith are necessary.

Although these traditional beliefs are held by most conservative Christians, liberal Christians reject the concept of Hell as a physical location and interpret it metaphorically, as a state of mind, or as a place where one is separated from God. The belief that God sends people to be eternally tortured is obviously not consistent with the idea of a loving God. As Tom Harpur states in his book, *Life After Death*, "Since it is a fundamental spiritual law that the worshipper becomes like the object of his or her worship, the worship of a deity assumed capable of eternally torturing billions of people has led to disastrous results." There is no consensus about the fate after death of (1) people in non-Christian countries who have never heard the Christian message and therefore have never been able to accept or reject it, (2) adults who have heard the Gospel message but have rejected it for whatever reason, (3) infants, or others who cannot understand the Gospel or make a rational decision to accept or reject it, and, (4) people who have not been baptized to absolve them of their "original sin."

Rapture: Many conservative Christians have expected Jesus's imminent return to Earth ever since the first century. They believe that when he returns, following Armageddon, the Kingdom of Heaven will be established, when all saved Christians who have died in the past will be resurrected. Both they and currently living saved Christians will rise toward Jesus Christ in the sky. This resurrection is called the Rapture.

In **Islam**, as in most religions, a good life is rewarded and a wicked life is punished in the hereafter. The Koran describes Heaven and Hell in great detail. "We have prepared for the wrongdoers a fire whose flaming canopy shall enclose them. And if they cry for help, they will be helped with water like molten lead which will burn their faces." The afterlife in Paradise is described as follows: "And He shall reward them . . . with Garden and a raiment of silk; reclining upon their couches, they will find neither excessive heat nor excessive cold . . . and its clustered fruits will be brought within easy reach . . . and there will wait upon them youths who will not age." In these days of jihad, the Muslim martyr is deluded into believing that he will be rewarded by many joys in Heaven, including a bevy of virgins. However, there is some doubt about the virgin quote from the Koran. Recent scholarly examination of the original text of the Koran, which was in an Aramaic-like language, rather than Arabic, indicates that the words in the Koran, "houris" with "swelling breasts" are actually "white raisins" and "juicy fruits" (Christoph Luxenberg, *Die Syro-Aramäische Lesart des Koran* (*The Syro-Aramaic Reading of the Koran*), Berlin: Verlag Hans Schiler, 2004. See also, *What the Koran Really Says*, ed. Ibn Warraq, Prometheus Books, 2002; also *Newsweek*, July 25, 2003).

The **Baha'i** religion, which is only about 150 years old, and therefore is not so encumbered with ancient religious dogma, also considers that a human soul is eternal. It enters a human body at birth in order to obtain enrichment by experiencing the wisdom of current prophets. Followers believe that in the afterlife Heaven and Hell are the result of good or bad conduct during a human's lifetime, but the Baha'i concept of these places is more benign than in other religions. Heaven is the achievement of a close relationship with God, and Hell is the absence of God's presence and benefit.

2.2.4 Naturistic Spirituality

In native and primitive religions, including Shinto and the religions of the American aboriginal peoples, spirituality resides in many forms, including animals, plants, and non-organic materials such as water, rocks and mountains. Living in harmony with nature is absolutely necessary, since natural things are an expression of the spirit of a Supreme Being (God). The spirit or soul of a human remains after death, and communion with ancestral spirits is important. Living a good life is important. Those who have led a sinful life will not go to Hell, but will feel sadness and shame. These concepts are much more forgiving and humanistic than those of the great modern proselytizing religions, such as Christianity and Islam.

2.3 Eastern Spirituality

The religions of Hinduism and its offshoot, Buddhism, have long fascinated Westerners, because of their ascetic, mystic and spiritual aspects. Who has not admired the Indian Guru, or spiritual teacher, who inspires his followers to live a more contemplative, serene, and benevolent existence? Many famous Westerners, including Sir Richard Burton, and more recently, the popular pop music group of the 1960s, the Beatles, have made the pilgrimage to India to discover the mysteries of the ascetic life. This fascination is perhaps a reflection of Western man's sense of loss, his pining for the purity of the ancient Christian tradition of monastic orders. He believes that the Eastern religions have retained their spirituality.

An additional reason for this interest in Eastern mysticism is disillusionment with the Western monotheist religions, which have been so corrupt and violent. Many westerners believe that the spiritual and meditative aspect of the Eastern ways is the reason that Eastern religions have avoided the bloody history of the monotheist religions. This belief may be justified.

2.3.1 Zen Buddhism

Buddhism originated when Siddhartha Gautama (the future Buddha), a prince of Northern India and a Hindu, experienced the "Four Sights," which illustrated the pain and suffering of the world. He decided to forsake his wealth and status, and to learn about the common man by wandering through India as a penniless beggar, as did many Hindu holy men at that time. After seven years, he paused to meditate under the famous Bo tree. There he achieved Supreme Enlightenment, and stated his First Law of Life, which is the Key to Wisdom: "From good must come good, and from evil must come evil." This is also the ancient Hindu Law of **Karma**.

The Buddha stated, "I teach only two things, O disciples, the fact of suffering and the possibility of escape from suffering." He believed that all human suffering was caused by desires, such as lust, greed, and envy. Man could control his desires by achieving a higher consciousness or enlightenment (**Nirvana**) through compassion, moderation, and meditation. The goals of Buddhism are wisdom (**prajna**) and love (**karuna**). Love is the vehicle through which wisdom is attained. The Buddha preached his new philosophical doctrine throughout India until his death at the age of about eighty. He declined the request of his followers to appoint a successor. In fact, he did not believe in religious authority or hierarchy, and encouraged his followers to seek their own spiritual way. He also did not believe in ritual, prayers, tradition, and speculation about an eternal soul. Unfortunately, later Buddhism did develop a hierarchy similar to that of other religions, and the Buddha was worshiped as a God, contrary to his teachings.

Buddhism, which spread rapidly through India, became the dominant religion there for several centuries. Finally, around 1100, Hinduism was reformed, and again became the major religion of India. In the meantime, Buddhism had spread to all of Southeast Asia, including China and Japan. The famous Indian teacher, **Bodhidharma**, introduced Buddhism to China around the year 475. The blending of his teachings with the more naturistic Taoism of China led to the humanistic **Chan** version of Buddhism, a form of Mahayana Buddhism. Around 1200, Chan spread to Japan, where it developed into a uniquely Japanese form called Zen. Its ideals of mental tranquility, fearlessness, and spontaneity have had lasting influence on the cultural life of Japan. In modern Japan, Zen has about ten million followers. Zen spread into Western countries in the latter half of the twentieth century.

The word Zen means meditation (chan in Chinese, **dhyana** in Sanskrit). Meditation is considered the most important feature of Zen Buddhism with the goal of enlightenment, achieved through intuitive understanding, or wisdom. In spite of the fact that Buddhism is basically a philosophy rather than a religion, it is in many ways more spiritual than the conventional polytheist and monotheist religions. The spirituality takes the form of meditation. Zen teaches that the potential to achieve enlightenment is universal, but remains dormant in most people because of ignorance. Enlightenment is attained, neither by the study of scripture, nor by the practice of good deeds, rites and ceremonies, nor by worship of images, but by a sudden inspiration, a departure from common, logical thought. Paradoxically, the best way to achieve enlightenment is to learn meditation from a Zen Master.

A famous dialogue of Zen is as follows. A monk asks a Zen master, "What kind of person can achieve enlightenment?" The master replies, "He is an ordinary man." The monk then asks, "What is a man like after becoming enlightened?" The master replies, "His head is covered with ashes and his face smeared with mud." The monk then wonders, "What does that mean?" The master replies "Not much, just so." The answer to the first question means that anyone can achieve enlightenment. The second answer means that an enlightened person strives for the welfare of humanity. The third answer reflects the humility of Zen.

The teaching methods vary among the various sects of Zen. The **Rinzai** sect, introduced to Japan from China by the priest Ensai in 1191, emphasizes sudden shock and meditation on the paradoxical statements called **koan**. The **Soto** sect, brought to Japan by Dogen on his return from China in 1227, prefers the method of sitting meditation (**zazen**). The **Obaku** sect was established in 1654 by the Chinese monk Yin-yüan (Japanese: Ingen). It employs the methods of Rinzai and also practices **nembutsu**, the continual invocation of **Amida** (the Japanese name for the Buddha).

Zen uses very formalized procedures for zazen meditation, including how to enter the meditation hall, the **zendo**, with proper bowing and greetings, how to place the hands, how to breathe, and so on. In the simple **Gassho** hand position, the hands are palm to palm, with the fingers pointing upward and the arms roughly parallel to the floor. In the **Hokkaijoin** position (cosmic mudra), the right hand is placed palm upward against the lower abdomen, the left hand is palm upward on top of the right, the second joints of the middle fingers are touching, with fingers parallel, and the thumbs are up with thumb tips touching lightly together to form an oval between the thumbs and fingers. The thumb tips should join at the approximate level of the navel. Perhaps these many ritual positions and formalities assist in preparing the body and mind for deep meditation.

Breathing during zazen is gentle and silent. On inhalation, the abdomen expands naturally like a balloon inflating, and on exhalation, it deflates. In some Rinzai and Tibetan teaching, it is recommended to feel a sense of strength in the abdomen while breathing. During meditation, thoughts are permitted to wander freely, and there is no effort to control them, or to concentrate on any particular object. Meditation can also be done while walking (**Kinhin**).

Zen Masters use the mysterious sayings called **koan** to illustrate that simple logic can be misleading, and that it does not assist in the attainment of wisdom, which is the basis of enlightenment. Some scholars have compared koan to the often-mysterious parables of Jesus Christ (see *Hear Then the Parable* by Bernard Scott). The Shakyamuni Buddha, 2,500 years ago, illustrated the Buddhist attitude toward the use of words. "Bodhisattvas (prospective Buddhas) never engage in conversations whose resolutions depend on words and logic." In other words, truth and wisdom are independent of words. Words may or may not contain truth. Ultimately, the awakening to our fundamental enlightened mind is beyond descriptions possible in words. Words are limited by the minds of both speaker and listener.

One well-known monk and scholar, Shen Xiu, wrote,

> The body is a Bodhi tree,
> The mind a bright mirror stand.
> Time and again wipe it clean,
> And let no dust alight.

An illiterate peasant composed a poem supposedly having more insight than that one.

> Originally, Bodhi has no tree,
> Nor the mirror any stand.
> Basically nothing can be;
> Where can dust land?

He became the Sixth Buddhist Patriarch (Huineng). This story reveals the split between the two conflicting ideas of how enlightenment might be achieved, through gradual learning and long contemplation, which is the old Indian method, or through sudden enlightenment, which is the newer, humanistic Chan (Zen) way. It also illustrates the nihilist ideals of Buddhism.

Feng Yu-Lan, a modern historian of Chinese philosophy, lists five Chan principles.

1. The Highest Truth is inexpressible.
2. Spirituality cannot be cultivated.
3. In the last resort, nothing is gained.
4. There is nothing much in Buddhist teaching.
5. In carrying water and chopping wood, therein lies the wonderful Dao (the way or path).

The Gateless Gate: The Gateless Gate is a collection of forty-eight koan, or short Chinese philosophical puzzles, which illustrate how to pass through the gate to enlightenment. It is a gateless gate, because there are a thousand ways to enter the path to Nirvana, or Enlightenment. The koan were assembled in 1228 by the Buddhist monk Mumon, in a Chinese monastery. He said,

> "The Great Way has no gate,
> A thousand roads enter it.
> When one passes through this gateless gate,
> He freely walks between heaven and earth."

Mumon commented "Those who cling onto words are fools who believe that they can catch the moon with a stick or can scratch their itchy foot through a leather shoe. How can they 'see' reality as it actually is?"

Here is one Gateless Gate koan, with Mumon's comments.

Joshu's Dog: A monk asked the Master Joshu, "Has the dog the Buddha nature?" Joshu replied, "**Mu!**" (Mu is the negative symbol in Chinese, meaning Nothing or No.)

Mumon's Comment: "For the pursuit of Zen, you must pass through the barriers (gates) set up by the Zen masters. To attain his mysterious awareness you must completely uproot all the normal workings of your mind. If you do not pass through the barriers, nor uproot the normal workings of your mind, whatever you do and whatever you think is a tangle of ghost. Now what are the barriers? This one word "Mu" is the sole barrier. This is why it is called the Gateless Gate of Zen. The person who passes through this barrier shall meet with Joshu face to face and also see with the same eyes, hear with the same ears and walk together in the long train of the patriarchs. Wouldn't that be pleasant?

"Would you like to pass through this barrier? Then concentrate your whole body, with its 360 bones and joints, and eighty-four thousand hair follicles, into this question of what 'Mu' is; day and night, without ceasing, hold it before you. It is neither nothingness, nor a relative 'not' of 'is' and 'is not.' It must be like gulping a hot iron ball that you can neither swallow nor spit out. Then, all the useless knowledge you have diligently learned till now is thrown away. As a fruit ripening in season, your internality and externality spontaneously become one. As with a mute man who had a dream, you know it for sure and yet cannot say it. Indeed, your ego-shell suddenly is crushed, you can shake heaven and earth. Just as with getting hold of a great sword of a general, when you meet Buddha you will kill Buddha. A master of Zen? You will kill him, too. As you stand on the brink of life and death, you are absolutely free. You can enter any world as if it were your own playground. How do you concentrate on this Mu? Pour every ounce of your entire energy into it and do not give up, then a torch of truth will illuminate the entire universe.

Has a dog the Buddha nature?
This is a matter of life and death.
If you wonder whether a dog has it or not,
You certainly lose your body and life!"

Not every Zen scholar agreed with Mumon's interpretation of this famous koan. Amban was a Zen master who said, "Master Mumon, the old Zen master, discussed forty-eight koan. He is just like a famous old donut seller who told the buyer to open his mouth and stacked the donuts in his mouth, so the customer neither could spit them out nor swallow them. Mumon thus annoyed everyone enough, so I, Amban, will fry for Master Mumon another donut in the hot sizzling oil. I will make a forty-ninth koan and will show it to the world by following in Master Mumon's footsteps. I wonder how Master Mumon will eat it? Should he be able to swallow it at once, a miracle will occur, like when the Shakyamuni gave a sermon, the world will be full of light and the earth will move. Should he fail to chew and swallow it, all these forty-eight Koans will turn into the fiery sands. Now, quickly answer it, quickly answer it."

It is interesting that the Great Cultural Revolution of communist China in the 1960s had its own version of humanistic Zen philosophy. Intellectuals and academics were scorned, the common man was elevated, and full human potential was supposed to be achieved by returning everyone to the land. All intellectuals and professional people were forced to labor in the fields with the peasants. This movement was a disaster. The principle of human equality was admirable, but the means of executing it was deplorable.

2.3.2 Shinto

Another Eastern religion that has retained its spiritual core is **Shinto**, an early naturist religion that has persisted to modern times. It is practiced by about 85% of the 128 million Japanese. According to popular (but erroneous) Japanese belief, Shinto is as old as Japan herself. It remains Japan's major religion, along with Buddhism. The name Shinto is a combination of two

Chinese words meaning "the way of the gods" (**shen** "spiritual power, divinity," and **tao** "the way or path"), first used at the beginning of the early modern period. The Japanese word is **kannagara**: "the way of the **kami**" (gods, or divine spirits).

Although the major kami of Shinto are the gods of creation, numerous sacred spirits that take the form of natural things such as wind, rain, mountains, rocks, trees, and rivers. Kami include all things that contain divinity, which may be anything in the universe that is wondrous or significant for human life. Believers feel they are controlled not only by the principal kami, but also by numerous ancestors, spiritual beings, and divine natural forces. Humans become spirits after they die and are revered by their families as ancestral spirits. In ancient times, individual tribes worshiped a single kami who was regarded as the founder or principal ancestor of the clan. When tribes conquered neighboring tribes, the victors' kami were adopted by their new subjects.

An ancient example of the creation of the divine from the ordinary involves an emperor who was riding his horse in a thunderstorm, and encountered a cat who waved a greeting to him from a porch. Intrigued by this clever cat, the emperor dismounted and approached the porch. As soon as he reached the porch, a bolt of lightning struck his horse and killed it instantly. After that, cats were worshiped in Shinto as protective kami. Even today, when patrons enter a Japanese restaurant, they will usually see a porcelain statue of the waving cat, which protects them from harm. Such mythical and folk aspects of spirituality bring it down to the human level and soften its esoteric aspects.

In the Shinto religion, people worship by praying at a home altar or at public shrines. On almost every corner of most cities and villages, it seems there is a small shrine, often devoted to a single kami. In many homes, an altar, the **Kami-dana** (Shelf of Gods), having a model of a holy shrine, is given a central place. A mirror is placed in the center, and gods are connected to the Kami-danas through these mirrors. **Origami** ("Paper of the spirits") is a Japanese folk art in which paper is folded into beautiful shapes. It is often seen around Shinto shrines. Out of respect for the tree spirit that gave its life to make the paper, origami paper is never cut. Originally, public shrines were pieces of unpolluted land surrounded by trees or stones. Now, there are many large shrines in Japan, which invariably contain beautiful gardens as well as large open buildings for worship. The gardens are places for contemplation and communion with nature, a very important part of the Shinto religion. At the entrance to the larger shrines are large **Tori** gates, through which worshipers must enter. They symbolize gateways into the spirit world of the kami. The prayer center of a Shinto shrine is usually a single room (or miniature room) raised from the ground and with objects representing kami placed inside.

Shinto prayer is based on the belief that spoken words have spiritual power. If spoken correctly, the prayer will produce favorable results. Often, worshipers at shrines pray for good health, business success, safe deliveries, traffic safety, good exam performance, and so on. The worshiper writes his prayers on small pieces of paper, which he ties to shrubs designated for this purpose. Many shrines are known for certain blessings, such as happy marriage, finding a mate, obtaining good grades at school, etc. A prayer and offerings to the gods by a high official of the Shinto religion is a common custom when building a new skyscraper. Before starting a new business, the owners check the Shinto calendar for a lucky day when the Gods will favor them.

In contrast to many religions, there are no absolutes in Shinto. There is no absolute right or wrong, and nobody is perfect. This principle could well be adopted by the dominant monotheist religions of the world. Shinto is an optimistic faith, as humans are thought to be fundamentally good. Evil is caused by evil spirits, consequently the purpose of most Shinto rituals is to keep away evil spirits by purification, prayers and offerings to the kami. Cleanliness is important and the gods are pictured as disliking disorder. The Shinto religion gives great importance to nature, purity, and tranquility. Nature, in its infinite power and beauty, is understood as the manifestation of divine power.

As with all religions, certain forces attempt to use religion to enhance individual or state power. In the Meiji period (1868-

1912), Shinto was made Japan's state religion. Shinto priests became state officials, important shrines received governmental funding, Japan's creation myths were used to foster an emperor cult, and Shinto was separated from Buddhism. During the Second World War, Shinto was exploited to promote Japanese nationalism and imperialism. The separation of Japanese religion from politics did not occur until just after World War II, when the Emperor was forced by the American occupying forces to renounce his divinity.

2.4 Gnosticism

Gnosticism predates Christianity, and later became a spiritual sect of early Christianity. It was a mystical, ascetic, pessimistic and dualistic religion that derived much of its dogma from Zoroastrianism. It was the basis for the powerful Manicheanism of the third and fourth centuries, and the strong Cathar movement of the eleventh and twelfth centuries. Elements of its creed, that all matter is corrupt, and that one must overcome evil desires and carnal lusts to attain the Kingdom of Heaven, remain in modern Christianity. Gnosticism allowed a very individualistic approach to spirituality.

Up to the fourth century, there seems to have been a competition for supremacy among three Christian sects: the Jewish Christians, under Jesus's brother James, the Gnostics, and the eventual winners, the Pauline Christians, originating with Saint Paul. Little direct evidence remains of authentic Gnostic rites and tenets, since history is written by the winners. Much of the information we have was written by Pauline Christian apostles and by Romans, who provided their interpretation of Gnostic beliefs. As stated in the *Encyclopedia Britannica*, 1910 edition, "Of the actual writings of the Gnostics, which were extraordinarily numerous, very little has survived; they were sacrificed to the destructive zeal of their ecclesiastical opponents." In recent years, some light has been shed on Gnostic ideas by the discovery of the Dead Sea Scrolls and the Nag Hammadi "unknown Gospels." These have prompted a renewed interest in Gnostic ideas and ideals. Many popular and historical books that contain some aspects of Gnostic faith have recently appeared, such as *Holy Blood, Holy Grail, The Da Vinci Code, The Pagan Christ,* and *The Gospel of Mary of Magdala.*

The Gnostics' concepts of God and the imperfections of humanity are subtly different from those of the mainstream religions. **Gnosis** is the Greek word for knowledge, but in Gnosticism, it means "revelation" rather than "knowledge." A basic tenet of Gnosticism is the idea that all matter is evil. Somehow, the world was corrupted, largely by the frailties of humans. Thus, the doctrine of Gnosticism is very similar to the Buddhist principle that most of man's problems arise from his lust and passion. The Zoroastrian dualistic concept of the eternal struggle between good and evil, represented by two Gods, dominated Gnostic thought. One precept was that Christ and the Devil were the two hands of God, Christ being the right hand, with power over Heaven, and the Devil being the left hand, with power over this earth.

The ultimate objective of human redemption was the separation of the spirit from the body, thereby achieving personal salvation. This could be achieved through asceticism, contemplation, prayer, ritual, and sacraments. Some rituals that would aid in the path to Heaven were baptism by water, fire and the spirit (for protection against demons), consumption of holy food and drink, recitation of sacred formulas and the names of the various demons. These rituals were a type of magic, which exerted power via the use of weird names, sounds, gestures, actions, and magic formulas. No Gnostic was complete without the knowledge of the formulas which defeated the hostile powers. Gnostics believed that even the Redeemer (Jesus) had to use these rituals to ascend to Heaven. The emphasis on rituals is a reflection of the usual human attempt to control individual freedoms by organization, promoting institutional power. This excessive ritualization may well have contributed to the downfall of Gnosticism. Today, the importance of similar ritual has persisted in the many Christian sacraments.

In the modern Pentecostal faith, "speaking in tongues" is a direct extension of the Gnostic ideas of uttering weird sounds and mysterious formulas to promote salvation. Gnostics attributed special importance to the vowels: alpha, epsilon, eta, iota, omicron, upsilon, and omega. Jesus and His disciples are supposed to have spontaneously uttered gibberish of vowels in the middle of sentences. Within the last few years, Gnostic collections of vowels have been studied by scholars such as Ruelle, Poirée, and Leclercq. Each vowel corresponds to one of the seven planets, and they represent the Ideal and Infinite. They also represent a musical scale, and many Gnostic pages of vowels are sheets of music. Members of one Gnostic sect, the Ophites, were particularly fond of cosmic diagrams, consisting of circles, squares, parallel lines, and other mathematical figures.

Most Gnostic scriptures were in the form of myths, which believers considered to be universal truths told as allegories. Gnostics believed that the Christian Gospels were allegories, and so should never be taken literally (as fundamentalists have done through the ages). In the Gnostic creation myth, there was first the One, the unknowable God, just as in Judaism, Christianity and Islam. From the One, other lesser gods or **Aeons** were created, usually in pairs. One of these pairs of gods was Sophia ("Wisdom" in Greek) and Jesus. The idea that Gods fell from Heaven to earth, bringing great powers and hostile forces, was adopted from ancient religions of the East. Sophia was one of these fallen gods, in this case a Mother Earth-Goddess. The Primeval Man (Jesus?) fights the power of Darkness as he descends, and must find Light in his spirit, so that he may ascend again. This idea relates to the ancient Egyptian Sun God who daily falls into darkness, only to rise triumphantly again in the morning.

In one myth, Sophia, fearing the loss of her life, as well as the Light of the One, tried to emanate on her own without her male counterpart. Consequently, the lion-faced Demiurge or lesser god appeared. He created the physical world. Sophia, however, managed to introduce spirituality to the world via the Serpent. She gave Gnosis (knowledge) to humans this way, which angered the Demiurge, who thought he was the sole creator of the universe and the exclusive ruler of this world. The "original sin," in a gnostic context, is rather the "original enlightenment." Gnostics believed that Seth, the third son of Adam, was introduced to the gnostic teachings by both his father and his mother, and that this knowledge was preserved throughout creation. The savior (Christ) was sent to earth to give man the Gnosis needed to rescue himself from the physical world and return to the spiritual world. Gnostics rejected the Old Testament and Judaism, since they identified the Demiurge with the God of the Old Testament. Some Gnostics identified the Demiurge with Satan, a belief which contributed to Christian animosity.

Gnostic salvation is not just individual redemption of a human soul; it is a cosmic process. It is the return of all things to their state before the flaw in the sphere of the Aeons brought matter into existence, capturing some of the Divine Light within the evil Material World. The freeing of the Light is the process of salvation. When all Light has left, the Material World will be destroyed, in the final Armageddon. Individual salvation consists of the return of a man's spirit to the spiritual World or **Pleroma**. There is no resurrection of the body. Gnosticism lacks the idea of atonement. The Gnostic Savior was a god, not a man, and he did not save man since there was no sin to be atoned for, only ignorance. It follows that Jesus did not subject himself to sufferings for the sins of man. He was a teacher and brought the world Truth, which alone can save.

From the beginning, Christian Gnosticism was opposed by the emerging Pauline Christian sect. The last words of the aged St. Paul in his First Epistle to Timothy are usually taken as referring to Gnosticism, which is described as "Profane novelties of words and oppositions of knowledge falsely so called which some professing have erred concerning the faith." St Augustine is perhaps the most important Christian figure who was influenced by Gnosticism. He was, in fact, first a Manichaean before he rejected that faith to become Christian. However, many of the Gnostic and Manichaean concepts remained in his mind-set, probably giving rise to his asceticism, and to his negative attitude toward women and sexual intercourse.

In the United States, Gnosticism persists, notably in the Church called Ecclesia Gnostica, and in an organization for studies of Gnosticism named the Gnostic Society (primarily in Los Angeles).

2.5 Sufism

Sufism was the most spiritual branch of Islam. It persisted much longer than is usual for a mystical and ascetic sect of a major religion. Sufism can be described as "spiritual experience through mystical intuition and bodily discipline." Initially, it was a form of escape from the domination of the **madrassas** (schools) of Islam. Sufi is derived from "suf," meaning garments of wool, which ascetics traditionally wore. Sufism emphasizes a fear of Hell, a search for God, and a mystical "oneness with God." According to the Koran, "God is closer to man than his own neck vein." Al Husain ben Mansur al-Hallaj, one of the most important Sufi historical leaders, was the patron saint of Persian Sufis. He was executed in 922 for his Sufi beliefs, especially his blasphemous statement "I am the Truth."

In early Sufism, solitary meditation and ritual repetition of the **dhikr**, or invocations, led to séancelike trances. Often, music was used in such séance meetings, which displeased the orthodox Muslims. Later, as Sufism became more popular, Sultans and viziers established convents, often in combination with the already established madrassas, for the teaching of Sufism. These were called **zawiya**, or the Persian **Khangah**. They were often huge establishments, which supported whole communities and even regions. The Sufi organization was hierarchal. Each **ekklesia** (church) had a **shaikh** as leader, who was supposed to be descended from earlier shaikhs. In the Middle Ages (1150-1500), there were many very influential Sufi "orders:" the Qadiril (named after Abd al-Qaladir al Gilani of Baghdad, who died in 1166); the Shadhili in North Africa, Egypt, and Arabia; and the Chishti in Persia and India. Later orders were the Khalweti in the Ottoman Empire; the Tijani in North and West Africa; and the Shiite Safavi order, which established the Safavid Shahs of Persia (Iran) in 1500. The Bektashi order was a strong rural movement. In northwest Africa, the Berber form of Sufism practiced the worship of saints, even during the lifetime of some saints called **marabouts** or holy men. The term Sufi was later replaced by the name **faqir** (poor brother) or its Persian equivalent, **dervish**. (For example, the "whirling dervishes" of modern Turkey.)

Sufism took over both the spiritual and economic life of Muslims. The centerpiece of Sufi dogma was **Wahdat al-Wujud**, the "oneness of all existence," based on Neoplatonic monism (belief in the unity of everything). The orthodox **Ash'arite** theology was modified by the idea that the human spirit emanates from God Himself, and therefore all empirical existence is an illusion, which should be obliterated and absorbed into the Eternal Reality. The supreme mystical experience was union with God, like the Gnostic ideas. The Spanish-Arab mystic Ibn al-Arabi (who died in 1240) developed this doctrine in an immense literary output. Also, Jalal al-Din al-Rumi's work, *Masnavi Mawlana Rumi*, has been called the Bible of later Sufism.

For those Sufis who felt that becoming one with God was arrogant, an alternate goal was becoming "the perfect man," or the perfect image of God, which was a less mystical goal. A third system of faith was based on the Zoroastrian "Light of Lights." By application of faith and discipline, the soul ascends through different levels, approaching the ultimate illumination of the soul. The Druze sect of Lebanon is a remnant of Sufism.

The Golden Age of Islam prevailed from 1300-1700, when the Ottoman Empire reigned supreme, and its science, culture, and tolerance greatly surpassed that of the Christian West. It is associated with the benevolent cooperation of Sufism with the more fundamentalist Ash'arism. In the eighteenth and nineteenth centuries, Muslim nations became dissatisfied with their power and economic progress, in comparison with their chief threat—the Christian nations of the West. The result was a return to more fundamental, conservative Islam, in the form of sects like the **Wahhabis** of Saudi Arabia. This movement led to the decline of Sufism, which had also fallen out of favor because of its excessive structure of mandatory rituals and sacraments. The study of Sufism gradually vanished from the madrassas. Jamal al-Din al-Afghani (1838-1897), a Persian Shiite, led the push for "purification of Islam," and saw Islamic unity as necessary to resist the rising power of the West. In cooperation with Shaikh Muhammad Abduh of Egypt (1849-1905), he tried to achieve a balance between reason and revelation, between the truth of nature and the truth of God as told in the Koran. This led to the **neo-Wahhabi** or modern **Salafi** reformist movement and to the militant Muslim Brotherhood. The Sharia law, which was originally only for family matters, was established as Muslim law. Now, this law has been mostly superceded by legislated secular law, although only Turkey has abolished it completely.

This shift in the Muslim faith toward more dogmatism and fundamentalism proved to be detrimental to the development of Islamic nations. It was a futile effort to stem the tide of Western power. It led to the suppression of women's rights, religious freedom, tolerance and secular education. Fanaticism and Islamic jihad, directed toward Western culture, were an inevitable consequence of this return to fundamentalism.

2.6 Modern Christian Spirituality

Until recently, spirituality has been disappearing in Christianity. The bane of spirituality is fanatic adherence to a rigid set of tenets or doctrines, which derive from holy scriptures. Christian fundamentalists believe that every word of the Bible is the literal truth from God. Most religious scholars believe that the Bible is an allegorical set of tales and myths, written to give people spiritual and moral messages. It should not be taken literally.

A major Christian tenet states that, according to the New Testament, Jesus Christ was the son of God and gave his life to redeem the sins of mankind. This dogma has permeated Christianity to the extent that it is the fundamental building block of the faith. It has been seriously questioned by modern scholars. In Christianity, as in other monotheist religions, only one ultimate divinity (God) exists. This Supreme Spirit, which can never be comprehended by mere mortals, is a rather remote and cold concept. In order to make the religion more accessible to ordinary people, Christianity developed the idea of the Holy Trinity, which people can relate to more easily. This concept was likely a major reason for the success of Christianity. The Holy Trinity consists of the Father, the Son, and the Holy Spirit. Jesus is believed to be the Son of God, and, in many ways, is the supreme God of Christianity. These three manifestations of God make him more understandable, and thus provide a more humanistic rather than esoteric faith. However, they do detract from a spiritual concept of the one supreme God because of the dilution of the supreme God into three entities. The Holy Trinity dogma has always caused controversy, and was only incorporated in official doctrine after the synod of Nicaea (in modern Turkey) in 325.

The Holy Trinity has its parallel in Hindu beliefs. In Hinduism, there are many incarnations or avatars of the Supreme God, Brahman, and Jesus is considered to be one of these. Hinduism also has a trio of Gods, Brahma, Shiva, and Vishnu. Christians also worship Mary, the mother of Jesus, and other spiritual figures, namely a multitude of saints. Similarly to the Shinto religion, these saints have special spiritual powers in certain areas of human endeavor.

As pointed out by Tom Harpur (*The Pagan Christ*), Alvin Boyd Kuhn (*A Rebirth for Christianity),* and others, the details of Jesus's life, including his virgin birth, many of his teachings, his death on the cross, and his Resurrection, are strikingly similar to those told in the ancient Egyptian religion, and specifically to those of its God Horus. (There are also many similarities with the lives of the Buddha and of Lord Krishna of Hinduism). The same story of Christ was related thousands of years earlier in Egypt. The Egyptian Christ was Horus, son of Osiris and Isis. The morning star, Sirius—like the Bible's star in the East—heralded the birth of Horus; Horus was baptized in the River Eridanus (Jordan) by Anup the Baptizer. Horus walked on water, cast out demons, and healed the sick. He was transfigured on a mountain, and he delivered a "sermon on the mount." Horus was crucified between two thieves, buried in a tomb, and resurrected after three days. He was called Iusu. Horus was the good shepherd, the lamb of God, and the fisher, like Jesus. He was the Way, the Truth, and the Life. Horus was supposed to rule for a thousand years, like Jesus. All the ancient sun gods had a life history gap between the ages of twelve and thirty, like Jesus. The age of twelve is that at which the ancients believed man realized he had a soul (Christian confirmation or

Bar Mitzvah age). Both Horus and Jesus were baptized at the age of thirty, which represents the age of full adult maturity. Both Jesus and Horus were accompanied by twelve disciples. Twelve is a very important number, being related to the twelve signs of the zodiac; also, twelve is the product of our three components—body, mind, and spirit—and the four elements of matter—fire, air, earth, and water. Note also the twelve tribes of Israel. In ancient religions of Egypt, Haldea, and Greece, there were the twelve rays of genius in man, represented by the twelve Reapers of the Golden Grain, the twelve Builders, the twelve Carpenters, the twelve Weavers, the twelve Fishermen, the twelve Sons of Jacob, etc.

In pagan times, these tales of a virgin birth, a martyr's death on the cross, and the Resurrection were intended to provide an allegorical spiritual message that the spirit of Christ (Christos) is within all humans. Taking these myths as literal truth destroys this message. St. Paul referred to Christos many times in his Epistles, but seldom to Jesus. He believed that everyone had divinity within. He wrote, "The spirit of God dwells in you." Assigning divinity to Jesus alone, as God's representative on earth, negates this powerful concept.

There are many other examples of dogmatic literal understanding of the words of the Bible, which detract from the spiritual message of Jesus. Some of these are the creation myth, "original sin," and the condemnation of the Jews for Jesus's death. They all erode the spiritual basis of Christianity. These misinterpretations were intended originally to sway the ignorant masses to the new Christian religion. The religious leaders of the first centuries of the Christian era knew what they were doing. They were successful in obtaining converts, but destroyed the central spiritual message of the myth of Jesus, which is that the suffering of man, like Jesus, in this material world, leads to a spiritual oneness with God. This is also the central tenet of Sufism.

Within religion, it is perhaps inevitable that spirituality comes into conflict with the more practical and power-seeking elements of the faith. In the early development of most religions, powerful spiritual sects existed, like the Gnostics of early Christianity, and the Sufis of Islam. Sects that emphasized the spiritual aspects of religion have always been, ultimately, suppressed by the mainstream elements, although they are often superficially tolerated. The Gnostics were completely obliterated by the "Pauline" Christians, whose ideas about the divinity and resurrection of Jesus dominate most Christian faiths today. Ironically, these ideas are in conflict with the teachings of Paul, who referred much more to "Christos," the mythical Christ symbol than to the man, Jesus. The legacy of the Gnostics has recently had somewhat of a resurgence with the discovery of the Dead Sea Scrolls in 1947 at Qumran, and the Nag Hammadi Scrolls (including the "unknown Gospels" of Mary Magdalen and Thomas) in 1945 in Egypt.

Sometimes, rather than fighting for the power base that is necessary for survival, spiritual sects respond to physical and moral threats by withdrawing to a monastic existence. The idea of leaving an unfriendly environment to commune more effectively with God in a secluded monastery on a mountaintop is one approach to life's threatening forces. There, man can commune with the spirits in peace. Of course, in much of the world today, each person can create a private monastery in his heart, without fear of persecution. In fact, recent polls indicate that the decline in church attendance in the Western world reflects an increase in private spirituality and prayer, which avoids the excessive control of organized religions.

The recent revival of spirituality in the western world includes fascination with eastern mysticism, Zen Buddhism, "New Wave" ideas, and the rediscovery of Gnosticism and naturist beliefs. The Pentecostal movement is the most rapidly increasing segment of Christianity. With its pseudo-spiritual ideas of "speaking in tongues" and its revivalist approach, it has captured the imagination of modern Americans who are dissatisfied with the overly hedonistic and materialistic modern world.

3

FANATICISM

A fanatic is one who can't change his mind and won't change the subject.—Sir Winston Churchill.

3.1 Introduction

In every religion, there are fanatics who practice their faith in an overzealous and intolerant manner. Most people believe that those who merely follow their religion in an obsessive way are not fanatics, so long as they do not offend or harm others. For example, religious sects that practice a solitary and monastic existence of prayer and contemplation do not usually present a threat to others, and in fact often have contributed considerably to art, science and religious thought. In contrast, religious fanatics believe that their religion is supreme, and insist on imposing it on others. In a completely illogical way, they consider that every word of their holy scriptures is the true word of God. For all holy writings, there are many versions, as these documents have been passed on orally, and have been translated (sometimes inaccurately) into many languages. Fanatics, in righteous zeal, often persecute, and sometimes kill those whom they perceive as having offended their faith. Examples abound. Consider the Spanish Inquisition, the Crusades, the Salem witch hunts, the Pogroms against the Jews, the massacres of Hindus and Muslims in India, and the suicide bombings of the recent Muslim holy wars or jihads.

Fanaticism is diametrically opposed to spirituality. Because the spiritual person is devoted to the mystic, divine aspects of the universe, he is less inclined to impose his beliefs on others. For this reason mystical sects are generally in the minority. Consider the Gnostics of Judaism, the Sufis of Islam and the various monastic orders of Christianity. Spirituality implies devotion to prayer and meditation, whereas fanaticism implies imposing an overly dogmatic and uncompromising view on others.

A major instrument of fanaticism is the religious cult (see Chapter 4). In modern terminology, cults are considered to be small religious groups that consist of devoted followers of a charismatic religious leader. The leader often demands unconditional and fanatic devotion to his commands, which frequently involve preparation for Armageddon and the Final Judgment Day. In some cases, such as the Heaven's Gate and the People's Temple cults, mass suicides of cult members occurred. These cults are on the surface not too much different from the cult of Jesus of Nazareth, who also predicted an imminent Final Judgment Day. Jesus's followers were also fanatically devoted to him, but in this case, the major religion of Christianity evolved from the cult. As discussed in Chapter 4, there is one main difference between self-destructive cults and mainstream cults that later evolve into religions. In the former case, the leader grows apart from his followers, and becomes an autocratic figure with self-seeking goals such as a luxurious lifestyle and perverted sexual privileges. In the latter case, the leader is regarded as a true prophet, leading his followers to spiritual and benevolent goals.

3.2 Abraham

Today, as always, there are many religious fundamentalists and fanatics who will kill on "the command of God." Unfortunately, they can refer to the example of Abraham, the father of the Judeo-Christian-Muslim faiths, who was prepared to kill his son to satisfy his God! How can anyone decide whether God's command to kill is a divine revelation, the delusion of an individual, or the power-lust of a religious leader? Here are some examples. A religious fanatic in the USA recently murdered a doctor who performed abortions. In his defense, he said that God commanded him to kill the doctor. Osama Bin Laden told his followers that it was the will of God to kill Americans and others whom he chose. The Ayatollah of Iran condemned the author Salman Rushdie to death for a book he wrote, in which Islam is, presumably, criticized. The Pope commanded his crusaders to kill Muslims to recover the Holy Sepulcher. Which of these actions are valid?

Abraham[5] was the founder of Judaism, as related in **Genesis**, which is the first book of both the **Torah** (the first part of the Hebrew Bible), and the Christian Old Testament. On God's command to "Go forth from your native land and from the land of your father's house to the land that I will show you," (Genesis 12) he led his people from near Ur, in Mesopotamia (now Iraq), to the Promised Land in Canaan, (now Israel and Palestine). In that land, God had promised Abraham that "I will make of you a great nation, and I will bless you."

Abraham is holy not only to Jews, but also to Christians and Muslims. Abraham is considered to be the father of Christianity, since he was the first to put his faith completely in the hands of God (**Yahweh, Jehovah**), to submit completely to God's will, as described in Genesis. In addition, Judaism forms the basis for Christianity, since the first five books of the Christian Bible are identical to the Jewish Torah. Also, Islam claims Abraham as its first prophet, even though he lived some 2500 years before Muhammad. Again, the major reason is the covenant that Abraham made with God, to lead his people to a new land, and, more importantly, to surrender himself completely to the one God. From Sura 16 of the Koran, "Abraham was a paragon of piety, an upright man obedient to God."

---

[5]   Note that the Bible refers to Abraham as "Ibri" (Hebrew), meaning "from the other side," because he came from the other (East) side of the Euphrates River. The word Israel (Hebrew: warrior of God) was the alternate name of Jacob, the grandson of Abraham. Consequently, his descendants became known as the children of Israel. The word Jew is derived from Judah (Hebrew: to be praised), who was the son of Jacob.

Abraham had two sons, first Ishmael, born from an Egyptian slave woman, Hagar, when his wife Sarah could not conceive, then later Isaac, born of Sarah late in her life. When Isaac was a few years old, Sarah decided that her son should be her sole heir, and commanded Abraham "Cast out that slave woman and her son." Astonishingly, Abraham obeyed, although reluctantly, banishing Hagar and Ishmael to the desert. (Islam believes that they were banished to Mecca.) God told Abraham to follow Sarah's command, but encouraged him by saying "As for the son of the slave woman, I will make a nation of him, too, for he is your seed." Ishmael is considered to be the father of the Arabs, and Isaac the father of the Jewish tribes. Later, as the ultimate sign of submission, Abraham was commanded by God to offer his son Isaac as a sacrifice, and Abraham was ready to obey. However, the command seems to have been only a test for Abraham, since at the last minute the angel of God said to Abraham "Do not lay your hand on the boy or do anything to him; for now I know that you fear God, since you have not withheld your son, your only son from me" (Genesis 22:12). Today, if a religious leader killed his son on the command of God, he would be labeled a religious fanatic, and would be convicted of murder.

3.3 Christian Fanaticism

Probably the world's most devastating and enduring racial and religious persecution was perpetrated by Christians against Jews. The Christian animosity toward Jews apparently originated with the crucifixion of Jesus, for which the Jews were held responsible. Christian leaders officially blamed Jesus's death on the Jewish people as a whole, and this condemnation persisted until very recently (1974). Christians also were angry that Jews did not recognize the divinity of Jesus. For these and other doctrinal reasons, in spite of the fact that Christianity is based on Jewish beliefs as written in the first five books of the Old Testament, various Christian leaders encouraged the persecution of Jews. Even Luther was strongly anti-Semitic, and the German Nazis often referred to his writings on the subject.

Jesus today would be considered a revolutionary leader, as well as a spiritual leader. He apparently believed that he was the Messiah[6], which meant that he was to be King of Israel. (Commonly, today, Messiah is thought to mean a spiritual leader only.) The Jewish prophecies for the future Messiah included his ancestry from David, his birth in Bethlehem, his triumphant arrival in Jerusalem on an ass, and his "cleansing" of the temple. The Gospels, written many years after Jesus's death, ensured the fulfillment of the first two of these prophecies, and Jesus accomplished the last two. According to the Gospels, he did arrive in Jerusalem on an ass, during the festival of Passover. His "cleansing" of the temple occurred when he ejected the moneychangers from the Jewish temple. The moneychangers were members of the Pharisee sect, to which Paul, and probably Jesus, belonged. It is also significant that Jesus instructed his followers to "acquire swords" (Luke 22:36). This was clearly an incendiary action.

The Jewish hierarchy was incensed by Jesus's behavior, and later was involved in the capture of Jesus before his judgment and crucifixion by the Romans under Pontius Pilate. Jesus was accused of claiming to be the "King of the Jews," which implied that he might incite the unruly Jerusalem crowds during the Passover festival. This was apparently reason enough for the Romans to arrest Jesus with a powerful military force of a "cohort" (about six hundred men), and later execute him by crucifixion[7]. According to the book of Matthew, the Jewish crowd demanded the crucifixion of Jesus, and then said, "Let his blood be on our

---

[6] From the Hebrew word, meaning "anointed one," referring to the traditional ceremony performed to inaugurate Jewish kings. Hence, the term Christ, from the Greek word Christos, "the Anointed," is applied to Jesus.

[7] There is some confusion about how many men the Romans used for the arrest. In the "Authorized Version" of the New Testament, "cohort" is incorrectly translated as "a number of men," which commonly meant only a few soldiers. This is an important point, as the use of a cohort of men means that the Romans considered Jesus to be a significant threat. (See *The Messianic Legacy* by Michael Baigent, Richard Leigh and Henry Lincoln, Arrow Books, 1996.)

heads and the heads of our children." Modern scholars believe that this scenario is unlikely since crucifixion was forbidden by Jewish law. They believe that the Gospel description of the involvement of the Jews in the condemnation of Jesus was overstated and inconsistent. This is likely because at the time of writing of the Gospels, some fifty years after Jesus's death, there was an ongoing struggle between the budding Christianity and Judaism. Also, at that time, the authors of the Gospels did not want to be too critical of the Romans, who were in control of Israel and had only recently in the year 70 crushed a major Jewish rebellion. Incredibly, although Jesus was a Jew, a later official Christian edict blamed the Jews of Jesus's day and all future generations of Jews for the death of Jesus. If Jesus was God's son, he had complete control over his destiny, and certainly would not have wanted his people, the Jews, to be persecuted for his willing self-sacrifice. For many centuries after, Christians persecuted and killed Jews (leading up to the horrific genocide, the Holocaust, during which the German Nazi regime killed some six million Jews from 1940-45). Only in 1974 did the Roman Catholic Church finally exonerate Jews from this fatal legacy. This persecution flagrantly violated the fundamentals of Christianity.

As an example of the inhumanity of Christian officials toward Jews, consider the following examples of events during the Holocaust. When thirty-five thousand Jews were sent from Slovakia to the Nazi death camps in 1942, a rabbi begged the Slovakian Archbishop Kametko to intervene to help the Jews. His response was "This is no mere expulsion. There you will not die of hunger and pestilence; there they will slaughter you all, old and young, women and children, in one day. This is your punishment for the death of our redeemer. There is only one hope for you—to convert all to our religion. Then I shall effect the annulling of this decree." (Quoted in *Why the Jews? The Reason for Antisemitism*, Dennis Prager and Joseph Telushkin, and attributed to Rabbi M.D. Weissmandel's autobiography *Min Hamezar*, p.24-25, cited in *Faith after the Holocaust*, by Eliezer Berkovits—also the following quote). Similarly, in 1944, Rabbi Weissmandel asked the papal nuncio to intervene to save Jews being sent to the Auschwitz concentration camp. The nuncio responded, "There is no innocent blood of Jewish children in the world. All Jewish blood is guilty. You have to die. This is the punishment that has been awaiting you because of that sin."

The Crusades (see Chapter 5. Power)

Quite often, religious or secular leaders incite the masses to fanatic religious behavior for motives of personal ambition. For example, Pope Urban II, in 1095, decided that he wanted to reunite the Roman Catholic Church with the Eastern Orthodox Church based in Turkey. He therefore answered an appeal for help from emperor Alexius I of Constantinople, who, in turn, wanted assistance in fighting the Muslims who had occupied the Holy Land of Palestine. The Pope cleverly incited the public to religious fervor in a dramatic speech, stating that he was commanded by God to free the Holy Sepulcher in Jerusalem from the heathen Muslims. Thus began the **First Crusade**, one of several over a span of 250 years. An interesting aspect of these wars is that, as always, each side felt that God was supporting them. The Christians promised forgiveness of all sins for those who died fighting the "infidels," and, undoubtedly, the Muslims did the same. Whatever happened to religious ideals and morals, for example, the Christian admonition to "love your enemy?"

3.4 The Assassins

Precursors of the present Islamic suicide bombers were the Assassins, the strike force of a Shiite sect in eleventh century Persia. Similarly to present-day religious fanatics, the Assassins were unwitting tools of their leaders, who exploited them to achieve personal power.

The Assassin strike force was developed by al-Hassan ibn-al-Sabbah around the year 1090. He was a Persian claiming descent from the Himyarite kings of South Arabia. He became a Muslim warlord, called a **Grand Master**, who occupied a strong mountain fortress at Alamut, strategically situated ten thousand feet above sea level, overlooking the shortest road between the shores of the Caspian Sea and the Persian highlands. From Alamut, al-Hassan expanded his domain by capturing other fortresses. He not only terrorized the caravan routes, but also formed a secret assassination organization, based on Shiite Muslim precursors, that trained the **fida'is** (the faithful) as assassins, probably using the narcotic hashish. This is the origin of the word assassin, which derives from the Arabic word **Hashshashin** or **Ashishin**, meaning hashish-user.

Marco Polo, who visited Alamut in about 1272, described the magnificent gardens and palaces built by the grand master at Alamut: "Now, no man was allowed to enter the Garden save those whom he intended to be his Ashishin. There was a fortress at the entrance to the Garden, strong enough to resist all the world, and there was no other way to get in. He kept at his Court a number of the youths of the country, from twelve to twenty years of age, such as had a taste for soldiering. Then he would introduce them into his Garden, some four, or six, or ten at a time, having first made them drink a certain potion which cast them into a deep sleep, and then causing them to be lifted and carried in. So when they awoke they found themselves in the Garden. When therefore they awoke, and found themselves in a place so charming, they deemed that it was Paradise in very truth. And the ladies and damsels dallied with them to their hearts' content. So when the Old Man would have any prince slain, he would say to such a youth: Go thou and slay So and So; and when thou returnest my Angels shall bear thee into Paradise. And shouldst thou die, I will send my Angels to carry thee back into Paradise" (from *The Book of Ser Marco Polo, the Venetian*, translated by Henry Yule, London, 1875).

The Grand Master Hassan used the weapon of assassination, or threatened assassination, as a very effective method of controlling those who opposed him. Even Sultans and their chief administrators, the Grand Viziers, were not safe. The assassination, in 1092, of the Grand Vizier of the Saljug sultanate, Nizam-al-Mulk, by a fida'i disguised as a Sufi, followed by several other murders, terrorized the Muslim world. Many attempts by caliphs and sultans to conquer Alamut failed, until finally the Mongol, Hulagu, destroyed the caliphate and seized the Assassin fortresses in 1256-1260. Since the Assassins' books and records were destroyed, information about this strange and spectacular order is limited.

One of the most famous Assassin leaders in Syria was Rachid-al-Din Sinan, who commanded the hill-fortress of Masyad and terrorized the Crusaders. He even threatened Saladin, the Sultan of Egypt, who was the eventual conqueror of the Crusaders. After the capture of Masyad in 1260 by the Mongols, the Mameluk sultan, Baybars, in 1272 finally destroyed the Syrian Assassin movement.

Today, descendants of the Assassin sect, who are Ismaili Muslims, a branch of Shiism, are scattered through northern Syria, Iran, Oman, Tanzania, and especially India, where they go by the name of Thojas or Mowlas. They all acknowledge as spiritual leader the Aga Khan of Bombay, who claims descent from Isma'il, the seventh Imam, through the last grand master of Alamut. The current Aga Khan, Karim, is the forty-ninth hereditary Imam of some ten million Shia Imami Ismaili Muslims, and is a direct descendant of the Prophet Muhammad through his cousin and son-in-law, Ali, the first Imam, and his wife Fatima, the Prophet's daughter. Prince Aly Khan, the father of Karim, had the reputation of being an international playboy—his second wife was the American actress, Rita Hayworth. He was bypassed as the spiritual leader of his sect in favor of his son, Karim, who is known for his philanthropic efforts. In recent years, his foundation, Aga Khan Development Network, has funded many health and educational projects, including the Aga Khan University in Karachi, Pakistan, which has recently dedicated a $300 million Faculty of Health Sciences. In 2005, Karim Aga Khan received the Andrew Carnegie Medal of Philanthropy.

The evolutionary transformation of the Muslim Grand Masters of Alamut, employing assassins to satisfy their lust for power, into philanthropic leaders of an influential Muslim sect, is an inspiring story of the ability of good to triumph over evil.

3.5 Islamic Jihad

Some people may believe that the modern Islamic jihad, or holy war against the USA and the West, initiated by Osama bin Laden in the late 1990s, and most noted by the infamous attack on the Twin Towers of New York on Sept. 11, 2001, is the natural culmination of the Assassin movement, or of the Crusades. Others may believe that the direct cause is the Western interference in Arab affairs because of the need for oil, or the Israeli-Palestinian conflict, or the invasions of Afghanistan and Iraq in 2001 and 2003. A major cause is likely the radicalization of Muslim religious schools called **madrassas**. (See "How the Holy Warriors Learned to Hate," By Waleed Ziad, published: June 18, 2004, in the New York Times newspaper.) The Islamic saying, "Jihad of the sword, like prayer, is a religious obligation," is not an ancient proclamation from Muhammad, but is less than twenty-five years old. It originated in Pakistani madrassas, which are a powerful source for propaganda against Western and Christian ways.

The **madrassas** in Pakistan and other countries today are run largely by the Wahhabis, the fundamentalist sect of Islam that governs the religious system in Saudi Arabia. Indirectly using money from the sale of oil to the West, the Wahhabis use the madrassas to teach their radical doctrine. The madrassas have been shown to act as training sites for terrorists. Even though only a small percentage of Pakistanis are educated in madrassas, and—according to one study—the majority of the terrorists who attacked Western nations from 1998-2004 had not attended madrassas, there is no doubt that many madrassas do teach fanaticism. The curriculum is based on radical Islam.

For centuries, madrassas were centers of Muslim learning, open to all classes of people. They taught not only Islam, but also law, the sciences, and administrative subjects. In the golden years of the Ottoman Empire, from 1300-1700, these schools contributed to the fact that Muslim science, culture and art flourished, and were far superior to Western achievements in that period. The madrassas were the school system in much of India before it was conquered by Britain in the nineteenth century. Unfortunately, the British destroyed the madrassa schools by establishing a colonial school system for wealthy urban children, in order to create "a class of persons, Indian in blood and color but English in taste, in opinions, in morals and intellect," as Lord Macaulay put it in 1835. This was the beginning of a sharp decline in madrassa education.

Many leading scholars, or **ulema**, were persecuted. In Delhi, madrassas were razed. The curriculum shrank, and, by the mid-20th century, most madrassas taught only a dogmatic version of Islam.

Various religious sects, representing Sunnis, Shiites, and Wahhabis, gradually took over the schools, in the hope of gaining political influence in India. When India was partitioned in 1947, one of these sects, the **Deobandi**, a Muslim revivalist and anti-imperialist group in Pakistan, began to call for "Islamization." Based on their interpretation of scripture, they demanded new laws, including the restriction of women's dress and forms of popular entertainment. From the 1950s to the 1970s, this sect unsuccessfully sought political power through the concept of "Islamic Democracy." Later, the Taliban movement of Afghanistan was based on Deobandi doctrine.

A turning point in madrassa power came with the Soviet invasion of Afghanistan in 1979. The West and its allies decided to treat the war as a religious struggle. While Pakistani religious leaders had little political power, they did have considerable influence over the madrassas in Pakistan's northwestern frontier region and in Afghanistan. Madrassas were converted into training grounds for "freedom fighters," or **mujahedeen**. Driven by religious fervor, and financed and armed by Western money, these poor students succeeded in driving the Russians from Afghanistan. Of course, the end of the civil war meant an end to the Western money. The leaders of the mujahedeen needed a new cause. The Persian Gulf war and the Palestinian intifada provided one—hatred of America and the Christian West. A religious Pashtun militia, which became the Taliban, used the mujahedeen to take over Afghanistan. Unfortunately for the Afghan people, the Taliban oppressed them with repressive Muslim Sharia laws, such as forbidding women to attend school or even to earn a living, and supported the terrorist, Osama bin Laden. The Taliban governed Afghanistan only from 1996 to 2001, when they were overthrown by a coalition of Northern Afghan tribes and the USA. But the madrassas remain powerful in many parts of Pakistan, and are fueling a Taliban resurgence.

The malignancy of Islamic jihad has now spread to many countries, largely because of religious and patriotic fervor inspired by Western (both Christian and Jewish) aggression against Muslim nations.

The only solution to the threat of religious fanaticism, such as the Islamic jihad against the West (they should, rather, oppose their own corrupt regimes) is a long process of education, enlightenment, and improved standard of living. Clearly, a secular school system is necessary, but first, the madrassas must be diverted from their jihad viewpoint. Providing Western money for new schools is not the answer. The desire and funding must come from within the Muslim states. For self-preservation, the autocratic rulers of the Muslim world must modernize and liberalize their education systems. Education is also the key to increasing the standard of living, following the examples of Japan, Korea, Taiwan, Singapore, and more recently, India and China.

3.6 Modern Jewish Fanaticism

Not only Muslims and Christians have been guilty of fanatical and terrorist acts. Jews, one of the most persecuted religious groups in history, have been guilty of that behavior as well. From early biblical history, we learn that Moses was given special powers by God to terrorize the Egyptians, via plague, locusts, and even the death of all first-born sons, in order to free the Jews. This tale is, in all likelihood, allegorical, but it illustrates the mind-set of the early Jews, who were a warlike lot. Their Jehovah was a tribal, cruel, and unforgiving God.

In recent times, Jews forced Palestinians from their homes after 1948, during the Jewish-Palestinian conflict, using terrorist acts such as small massacres. Recently, in the military campaign against armed Palestinian groups, radical rabbis have encouraged the Israeli Army to kill Palestinian civilians. In a letter to Shaul Mofaz, the Israeli defense minister, the rabbis stated that killing enemy civilians is "normal" during the time of war and that the Israeli occupation army should never hesitate to kill non-Jewish civilians. A prominent rabbi, Dov Lior, in the Jewish "settlement" (enclave in the occupied territories) of Kiryat Arbaa near Hebron, stated that non-Jewish civilians may be killed to save Jewish lives—both soldiers and civilians—saying that "it is very clear in light of the Torah that Jewish lives are more important than non-Jewish lives." In 1994, after Baruch Goldstein, a Jewish "settler" killed twenty-nine Arab worshipers while they were praying at Hebron's Ibrahimi Mosque, Rabbi Lior praised him as a "great saint." (See "Cave of the Patriarchs Massacre," Wikipedia.org; and "Heil Druckman!" by Michael A. Hoffman, RevisionistHistory.org.) Ultra-orthodox Jewish settlers in the occupied areas of Palestine believe that they have a duty to occupy all the ancient biblical lands of Israel and Palestine, and some are prepared to die for that cause. Although most Conservative and Reform rabbis do not agree with Orthodox and Ultra-orthodox views, they have relatively little religious influence in Israel. The majority of Israelis do not condone violence and seek a reasonable solution to the Israel-Palestine dilemma.

3.7 Conclusions

There will always be religious fanatics. They believe that only their version of religion is the correct one and that other viewpoints must be ruthlessly suppressed. There will always be a few secular and religious leaders who exploit ignorant fanatics for personal or institutional power. These leaders, whether religious fanatics themselves, or merely cynical exploiters of fanatics, use religiosity for selfish purposes. Some claim to be spiritual leaders. Westerners criticize the extreme Ayatollahs of Islam, but must look also to their own religious fanatics, and to their own prejudicial religious beliefs. When the Pope of the Roman Catholic church says that the only way to salvation is through Jesus, he also errs. When the American people adulate fanatical "religious" leaders like Jerry Falwell or Pat Robertson, they also promote fanaticism.

Universal secular education is the key to the reduction of religious fanaticism. Religious schools, by their very nature, teach religious prejudice, which ultimately leads to religious fanaticism. Secular education, through most of the world, has aided in the spread of religious tolerance, but clearly more significant progress is needed. Even in the USA, which presumably has one of the best educational systems in the world, religious prejudice abounds. All schools should provide instruction about the world's religions, to show students that each religion has it own merits and is worthy of respect. When everyone believes that the spirit of God is within every individual, then all religions will be accepted.

4

CULTS

We don't know yet about life, how can we know about death?
—Confucius.

4.1 Introduction

Since most religions begin as cults, it is instructive to examine the origins, beliefs and structures of cults. The overwhelming inspiration of a cult is its leader. If the cult has an inspiring, selfless, spiritual leader, it may eventually become a sect, and then a religion. This happened with Abraham, Moses, Jesus, the Buddha and Muhammad. Most often, cult leaders are power-seeking fanatics, and the cult soon vanishes, sometimes with disastrous loss of life, as with doomsday cults.

Religious cults have been defined simply as systems of religious belief, or as groups that follow a religious system. In his book, *The Social Teaching of the Christian Churches*, Ernst Troeltsch classified religious groups as cults, sects, and churches, in order of increasing size. For Troeltsch, the cult represented a mystical or spiritual form of religion that appealed to intellectuals and the educated classes. Now, cults are considered to be small religious groups that deviate from the normal religious mainstream, and that consist of devoted followers of a charismatic religious or pseudo-religious leader. Most modern cults emphasize a familylike association, and a strong spirituality. The cult is a sort of religious island that gives followers a sense of belonging to a righteous, closely knit group, giving meaning to their lives. Often, cults believe in Armageddon and the Final Judgment Day, which, in some cases, leads to self-destructive behavior. Cults are challenges to conventional society, and often their dangers are overstated, because of some evidence of physical and sexual abuse of cult members, as well as brainwashing to convert new cult members. Sometimes parents have forcefully removed their children from cults, leading to judicial proceedings.

All cults evolve in a similar way. First, a few individuals are attracted to a benign and charismatic leader, perhaps because they lack self-esteem or a social support group, or because they are unsatisfied with their spiritual life. The group becomes self-sustaining because of the emotional bonds that develop among the members. As the cult grows, the power and influence of the leader becomes significant to society. The group continues to grow to the point where formal organization becomes necessary. The cult may establish businesses and become a tax-free charitable organization. The next stage is crucial. The leader may direct the efforts of his followers to beneficial goals, and a true sect or religion will develop. Alternatively, impressed by his success and by the adulation of his converts, he may begin to believe that he is a prophet, and in some cases even divine, and above secular law. This is the beginning of a disastrous sequence of developments. The leader grows apart from his followers, and establishes an inner core of power-seeking organizers. Often corruption occurs, and the funds of the cult are siphoned off to support a luxurious lifestyle of the ruling elite. (This may sound like the development of some mainstream churches). Or, the cult develops along Doomsday directions, and the leader predicts when the Final Judgment Day will occur. (The Gnostics followed this path). This is potentially the most dangerous development, as cult members often will follow their leader without question, since they believe that his wisdom is divine. Sometimes, mass suicides are the result, as happened with the Heaven's Gate and People's Temple cults.

Christian biblical sayings are often used to attract cult members. They are told that if they make sacrifices and give up everything to follow the true, righteous path (determined by the cult leader), they will be the "chosen ones" who will survive after the Second Coming of Jesus. A typical quote is from Matthew 16:24-26: "Then said Jesus unto his disciples, If any man will come after me, let him deny himself, and take up his cross, and follow me. For whosoever will save his life shall lose it: and whosoever will lose his life for my sake shall find it. For what is a man profited, if he shall gain the whole world, and lose his own soul? Or what shall a man give in exchange for his soul?" Similarly, from Matthew 10:38, "And he that does not take his cross, and follow after me, is not worthy of me;" and from Matthew 22:14, "For many are called, but few are chosen." Cult members are encouraged to leave their families in favor of the cult, inspired by biblical verses like, "And another of his disciples said unto him, Lord, suffer me first to go and bury my father. But Jesus said unto him, follow me, and let the dead bury their dead." (Matthew 8:21-22); and "He that loves father or mother more than me is not worthy of me; and he that loves son or daughter more than me is not worthy of me." (Matthew 10:37). Cult followers are also instructed to give their wealth to the cult, in accordance with the biblical saying, "Jesus said unto him, If thou wilt be perfect, go and sell that thou hast, and give to the poor, and thou shalt have treasure in heaven, and come and follow me. But when the young man heard that saying, he went away sorrowful, for he had great possessions. Then said Jesus unto his disciples, Verily I say unto you, that a rich man shall hardly enter into the kingdom of heaven. And again I say unto you, it is easier for a camel to go through the eye of a needle, than for a rich man to enter into the kingdom of God." (Matthew 19:21-24).

Most cults do not survive more than a few years. But many do develop into sects and even new religions. Religious orders such as the Franciscans began as cults under charismatic leaders who advocated lifestyles dedicated to advanced spirituality. The Mormon cult almost did not survive, as it was persecuted and driven from its chosen geographic area twice before settling in a remote part of the American West (now Utah), where it was free to develop into a sect, and eventually into a church. The

Cathars and Anabaptists of Europe began as cults, evolved into strong sects, but eventually were persecuted and annihilated by the powerful Roman Catholic Church. Lutherans started in a similar insecure way, but eventually prevailed to become a major church. Scientology started as a cult, and has evolved into a sect in some countries, but is still considered a cult in others. A cult becomes a sect when the number of followers is such that the group has considerable religious, social and political influence.

It can be argued that almost all sects and religions originated from religious cults. Initially, the followers of Jesus of Nazareth constituted a cult around him as a miracle worker. Later, the cult became a recognized Jewish sect. Only after a long internal struggle among competing Christian sects, over a period of centuries, did the present form of Christianity emerge as a major religion. Similar evolution from cult to sect to religion (or church) occurred in the cases of Buddhism and Islam. Each of the leaders of these three cults, Jesus, the Buddha and Muhammad, demanded that his followers adhere to a new set of morals. Modern cult leaders do the same, and exercise supreme control over the lives of their followers.

A brief summary of modern cults follows. The emphasis is on pseudo-Christian cults. They are divided into quasi-acceptable cults (those that do not seriously harm their followers or others), and doomsday cults, that have had fatal outcomes.

4.2 Quasi-acceptable Cults

4.2.1 Children of God (The Family)

The Children of God cult was founded in 1968 in California, USA, by a former Christian Missionary Alliance pastor, David Brandt Berg (1919-1994)—known within the group, variously, as Moses-David, Mo, Father David, or Dad. It was part of the Jesus Movement of the late 1960s, with many converts drawn from hippie groups. In 1978, because of reports of financial mismanagement, child abduction, and sexual abuse—complaints which were factors in the anticult movement of the 1970s and 1980s in the United States and Europe—Berg reorganized the Children of God and renamed it the "Family of Love," and later, the "Family" and the "Family International." Over a period of twenty-four years, Berg wrote a series of about three thousand published "Mo Letters" to his followers. These letters formed the basis of the cult. After his death in 1994, his widow, Karen Zerby, became the leader of the Family. At the beginning of 2005, there were 1,238 communal houses (Family Homes) and 10,202 members worldwide.

In 1974, the cult introduced a method of evangelism called "Flirty-Fishing," which allowed female members to physically express God's love by engaging in sexual activity with potential converts. According to the Family, as a result of Flirty-Fishing, "more than 100,000 received God's gift of salvation through Jesus, and some chose to live the life of a disciple and missionary." Children born as the result of Flirty-Fishing were referred to as "Jesus Babies." By the end of 1981, more than three hundred "Jesus Babies" had been born. Flirty-Fishing was officially abandoned in 1987. Sexual contact with nonmembers and with children was forbidden under penalty of excommunication. This policy was not retroactive.

In a 1995 court case in Britain, Justice Ward ruled that the sect, including some of its leaders, had sexually abused minors and subjected them to severe corporal punishment. However, he concluded that the Family now offered a safe environment for children. He did require that the sect cease all corporal punishment of children in the United Kingdom and denounce any of Berg's writings that were responsible for sexually inappropriate behavior. The January 2005 murder of a former member by the leader's stepson, Ricky Rodriguez, a "Jesus baby" who had left the group several years earlier, and Rodriguez's subsequent suicide, led to considerable media attention.

Theologians consider that the Family's basic theology conforms to Christian tradition. Leaders of the Family International believe that the Bible is the inspired Word of God. David Berg is regarded as a prophet, who passed on the message of God. They believe his "mantle" passed to his wife, Karen Zerby, at his death. They regard the officially published writings of both of them, but not everything they have written, as part of the Word of God. They believe that evangelizing and the service of God are the duty of every Christian. A central tenet is the "Law of Love," stating that if a person's actions are motivated by unselfish love and are not intentionally harmful to others, they are in accordance with Scripture and the eyes of God. They believe that this tenet supersedes all other biblical laws. They say that God created human sexuality, that it is a natural emotional and physical need, and that heterosexual relation between consenting adults of legal age is a pure and natural wonder of God's creation, permissible according to scripture.

Family members believe that they are now living in the period known in scripture as the "Last Days," the era immediately preceding the return of Jesus Christ. In that period, the world will be ruled for seven years by the Antichrist, during a time of persecution and disasters called the Great Tribulation. At the end of this period, following the "Battle of Armageddon" between Jesus and the Antichrist, believers will rise to heaven in an event known as the "Rapture," and Jesus Christ will reign on Earth for a thousand years.

The Family is a typical cult, illustrating the cult characteristics of communal living, fanatical devotion to a charismatic leader, belief in "Rapture," and (sometimes) sexual abuse of children. In this case, no disastrous mass suicides have resulted from their belief in the imminent Armageddon. Because of this, and because they have repented some of their earlier sexual sins, this cult is considered quasi-acceptable.

4.2.2 Christian Science and Scientology

Christian Science and Scientology are now accepted, more or less, as genuine Christian sects. They have some positive aspects and have advanced beyond being dominated by their original charismatic leaders. Nevertheless, they deviate so much from the mainstream of Christian beliefs that they could still be considered cults.

Christian Science is a spiritual movement, based on the writings of Mary Baker Eddy, chiefly her book *Science and Health with Key to the Scriptures*. A major part of the book is the power of faith healing. Christian Scientists believe that all of matter is illusory (similar to Gnostic beliefs), and that evil, disease and suffering are also not real. Only God exists. God is the supreme and only power. He is a loving God. Jesus existed to lead man to a belief in God. Death does not exist, as the human soul is immortal. Since suffering and disease are not real but are the result of fear, ignorance, or sin, it follows that they can be overcome by prayer and trust in a loving God. Standard medical practice is not condemned, but followers are encouraged to avoid it in favor of prayer. The combination of normal medical treatment and Christian Science prayer is not recommended. Of course, these beliefs have caused some conflict with secular law, which frowns on faith healing, at least in cases of potentially fatal illnesses. Students of Christian Science are usually members of the Church of Christ, Scientist.

The Church of Scientology, commonly called Scientology, has had a rather stormy history. It was established by the science fiction writer, L. Ron Hubbard in 1952. It is based, in large part, on Hubbard's 1950 book, *Dianetics: The Modern Science of Mental Health*. Scientology describes itself as a religious nonprofit organization dedicated to the rehabilitation of the human spirit, and one that provides counselling and rehabilitation programs. Followers claim that its teachings have cured them of addictions, depressions, learning disabilities, mental illnesses, and various physical ailments such as arthritis and cancer. For some time, Scientology was banned in several countries, most notably Germany. One reason is that it seemed to be a business enterprise rather than a nonprofit religious sect, because of the sale of certain items to converts. Scientology pays members commissions on new recruits they bring in, so Scientology members routinely try to "sell" Scientology to others. Scientists, medical doctors, and psychiatrists have described Scientology's ideas as pseudoscience. Consequently, Scientology is frequently classified as a cult or a pseudoreligion.

Some central beliefs of Scientology are these: (1) every person is an immortal spiritual being or **thetan**, who possesses a body and an eternal soul; (2) by the Scientology process of "auditing," a person can free himself of "engrams" and "implants" to reach more advanced states called "Clear," and "Operating Thetan," which reactivate natural spiritual abilities and physical well-being; (3) a person is basically good, but becomes "aberrated" by moments of pain and unconsciousness in his or her life; (4) truth is attained by observation and so-called truths established by others should not be forced on anyone; (5) psychiatry and psychology are evil and abusive. The main cleansing or "auditing" process in Scientology is done by a Scientology counsellor, who uses an E-meter, a device that measures very small changes in electrical resistance through the human body to determine previous traumatic events for the convert. This seems to be an extremely questionable procedure. Scientology literature includes many references to extraterrestrial past lives of thetans. This has an eerie resemblance to the sad case of the Heaven's Gate suicidal cult (Chapter 4.3.1.)

Scientology has become popular among some famous entertainment figures, such as Tom Cruise. It is common for those in the entertainment business to become enamored with a new cult or sect. They seek a spiritual outlet to balance their highly commercialized activities. They then become instant experts in areas where they have little or no knowledge. For example, Tom Cruise has become a self-appointed expert on psychiatry, which he considers, as does his sect, to be a pseudoscience.

Scientology claims to be fully compatible with all existing major religions. There are approximately fifty-five thousand Scientologists in the United States, according to data published by the U.S. Census bureau. The worldwide number of adherents is disputed. The Church of Scientology claims between nine and ten million followers, while the Web site, adherents.com, suggests there may be five hundred thousand.

4.2.3 Unification Church (Moonies)

This cult is based in Korea, under the leadership of Reverend Sun Myung Moon. Members are irreverently called

Moonies. As with many other cults, the charisma of its leader and his inspirational message were so strong that people felt obliged to leave their families and former lives to join the cult. Wives left their husbands and were subsequently married in mass ceremonies, in which hundreds of couples were united with mates of Reverend Moon's choice. The television program, Dateline NBC of July 16, 2004, explored one outstanding example of the control that this cult had over its members. The first child of one of these arranged marriages was supposed to be "blessed," and was taken from its parents to live and be educated in Korea. Needless to say, the results of this action were detrimental for the mental health of both the parents and the child, contrary to the goal of the Unification Church. There are now only about five thousand members of this movement in the USA, but perhaps hundreds of thousands worldwide.

4.2.4 Polygamist Cults arising from the Mormon Church

The Church of Jesus Christ of Latter-day Saints (LDS or Mormon Church), originated by Joseph Smith, and later led by Brigham Young in the Utah territory, practiced polygamy, and, indeed, considered it to be a requirement for exaltation and salvation. In 1890, the Mormon Church renounced polygamy, largely as a condition to gain the statehood of Utah. However, dozens of polygamous cults have been founded by disgruntled former Mormons in recent years, as offshoots of the Mormon Church. Two of these are **The Fundamentalist Church of Jesus Christ of Latter-day Saints (FLDS)** and **The True and Living Church of Jesus Christ of Saints of the Last Days (TLC)**. Such cults have been tolerated for decades, probably because their polygamous ways were not considered to be too offensive in the presently permissive society, and because it is difficult to prosecute religious groups for their beliefs. It has become apparent, however, that polygamy is not the only issue. There are the associated problems of subjugation of women, forced underage marriages, statutory rape, and corruption. It seems that these cults are an excuse to practice misogyny, corrupt patriarchal rule, and sexual misbehavior, rather than to practice religion. Furthermore, the inbreeding arising from decades of such polygamous behavior is leading to disastrous deterioration in local gene pools.

Salt Lake City writer John Llewellyn, a former fundamentalist Mormon, says, "The key factor in controlling a polygamist cult is in brainwashing the young women to inculcate upon their impressionable minds that everything not condoned by the prophet is evil, that they cannot go to the celestial kingdom unless they live in a plural marriage, and that the gates of heaven will be closed to the disobedient." (See Suzan Mazur "Seven brides for one brother: Plural marriage is rife in the western United States," *Financial Times*, 2000, also www. religioustolerance.org)

The FLDS cult was established in 1935 by two excommunicated LDS members. The church currently practices "The Law of Placing," under which all marriages are assigned by the prophet of the church. The cult is being investigated by police in both Utah and British Columbia for underage marriages, fraud, and racketeering. Warren Jeffs is the present leader of this cult. He took over when his father, the former leader, died in 2002, and he appropriated most of his father's wives. It is estimated that he now has about forty wives. Criminal charges were filed against him in 2005, and in 2006, he was put on the FBI's Ten Most Wanted list, for sexual assault on a minor. Later, in 2006, he was arrested.

The TLC cult was organized in 1994 by James Hampton because he believed that the LDS church was in apostasy. The True and Living Church claims to have restored the gospel truths of Joseph Smith in his founding of the Mormon Church, including plural marriage, consecration, and rebaptism. The TLC Law of Consecration requires members to consecrate all their possessions to the church. The TLC also believes in a form of reincarnation known as Multiple Mortal Probations. Cult members believe that Armageddon is near. The TLC has this to say about plural marriage: "We believe and live Plural Marriage because it is a commandment of God, and we fear God more than man. In living our beliefs, we do not break any enforceable laws. We do not obtain marriage licenses for successive marriages, and so are not guilty of bigamy. The only manmade law that is breached is that of 'unlawful cohabitation,' of which an immense number of citizens of the U.S. and other countries, who merely live together and copulate, are likewise guilty, thus rendering the law unenforceable."

4.2.5 Hare Krishnas and other Hindu cults

The Hare Krishna movement was an important part of the religious culture in North America in the 1960s and 1970s, where followers could often be seen collecting alms in the streets of large cities. It is an offshoot of Hinduism that worships Krishna as the supreme God. Unfortunately, as often happens in such cults, the leaders became obsessed with controlling all aspects of their followers' lives. Because members were supposed to be completely devoted to proselytizing and collecting alms, their children often were taken from them and sent to boarding schools, sometimes far away in India. There, the children were sometimes abused, both physically and sexually.

Some Hindu gurus, such as Bhagwan Shree Rajineesh of the Rajineeshee sect and Sai Baba are considered by their followers to be living embodiments of God.

4.3 Doomsday Cults

4.3.1 Heaven's Gate (flying saucers)

Heaven's Gate was a doomsday cult located in San Diego, California. The cult was founded by Marshall Herff Applewhite in 1993, originally, under the name "Total Overcomers Anonymous." (In 1975, he had organized a similar cult, called "Human Individual Metamorphosis"). In 1997, almost all of the cult members—a total of thirty-eight-committed suicide, believing that they would be transported, at death, to a spaceship where they would evolve to a higher level of existence. Since the cult members were highly educated, intelligent people, it is odd that they adopted such bizarre beliefs.

As in many doomsday cults, the members of Heaven's Gate believed that they were the chosen few who would survive Doomsday. They thought that certain passages in the Christian book of Revelation meant that UFOs (Unidentified Flying Objects) had visited earth about two thousand years ago, and that two witnesses of the event were killed, remained dead for three days, and then were resurrected and taken to Heaven. Two of the extraterrestrials on the spaceship were called "Do" and his female "Heavenly Father," called "Ti." They believed that Do came to Earth as a spirit that occupied the body of Jesus. Applewhite believed that he was a new Do, and that human bodies were only " . . . the temporary containers of the soul. The final act of metamorphosis or separation from the human kingdom is the disconnect or separation from the human physical container or body in order to be released from the human environment." The cult members believed that UFO's were spaceships operated by extraterrestrial beings who were trying to bring humanity to a higher level of knowledge. They were convinced that, by committing suicide together at the correct time, their souls would leave their containers (bodies) behind and would sleep until they were "replanted" in new containers. Eventually, their souls would be grafted onto representatives of the "level above human," who would be on a spaceship hidden behind the Hale-Bopp comet. The timing of the suicide was apparently triggered by the arrival of Easter and by the closest approach to earth of the comet, which they regarded as a celestial "marker." They feared persecution, death, arrest, physical torture, or psychological torture if they remained on earth.

The Heaven's Gate members lived communally in their "monastery" in San Diego. They abandoned their families, and became celibate. Eight of the group were castrated in preparation for the next life. The cult operated a World Wide Web business called "Higher Source" that designed web pages. Some of the surviving members still have a Web site called HeavensGate.com, from which some two hundred hours of audiotape and twenty hours of videotape of their beliefs can be downloaded. Their Web site was taken over by the FBI, but some individuals were able to download the site files and create mirrors at various locations. They will even send CDs of this material free of charge to those willing to pay shipping charges.

From their Web site:
"Whether Hale-Bopp has a 'Companion' or not is irrelevant from our perspective. However, its arrival is joyously very significant to us at Heaven's Gate. The joy is that our Older Member in the Evolutionary Level Above Human (the "Kingdom of Heaven") has made it clear to us that Hale-Bopp's approach is the 'marker' we've been waiting for—the time for the arrival of the spacecraft from the Level Above Human to take us home to 'Their World'—in the literal Heavens. Our 22 years of classroom here on planet Earth is finally coming to conclusion—'graduation' from the Human Evolutionary Level. We are happily prepared to leave 'this world' and go with Ti's crew."

Heaven's Gate is described by Jacques Vallee, in *Messengers of Deception: UFO Contacts and Cults,* Ronin Publishers (1979.) See also *The Gods Have Landed: New Religions from Other Worlds,* James R. Lewis, Ed., State University of New York Press, Albany, NY (1995.)

4.3.2 The People's Temple (Jim Jones)

The People's Temple was a doomsday cult founded by James Warren Jones (1931-1978) in the 1950s. He seems an unlikely candidate to become leader of such a radical cult, as he had graduated from both Indiana University and Butler University, and he was ordained in a mainstream Christian sect, the Christian Church/Disciples of Christ. The fate of the People's Temple cult is a good example of how a well-intentioned movement can lead to a Doomsday calamity. Jones's cult started off well. It was initially formed to aid the sick, homeless and jobless, and had over 900 members in Indianapolis during the 1950s. It was an interracial group, which was very unusual at that time. What transformed the cult into such a radical group? As Jones became more powerful within his cult, he assumed dictatorial powers, became paranoid, demanded complete obedience and devotion from his converts, and ultimately asked them to give up their lives. Most of them, perhaps weakened by starvation and sickness, apparently obeyed his call to suicide.

An important development for the cult was Jones's decision to move the cult to Ukiah, a remote town in Northern California. One possible reason for this move was a government investigation into Jones's "cures" for cancer, heart disease and arthritis. The second was his prediction of the imminent end of the world in a nuclear war. Ukiah was considered relatively remote from nuclear conflict. The cult later moved to San Francisco and then Los Angeles. A 1977 magazine story in the "New West," which suggested illegal activities within the Temple, caused Jones to move part of the cult to Jonestown, Guyana, where he had leased almost 4,000 acres of jungle. There, the cult established a commercial cooperative, called the "Peoples Temple Agricultural Project." Jones developed a belief called "Translation" in which he and his followers would all die, and would move to another planet for a life of bliss. Mass suicides by drinking poison were rehearsed.

At this time, Jones abused prescription drugs and became increasingly paranoid. Rumors of human rights abuses circulated. Tim Stoen, the Temple attorney and assistant to Jones, left the cult, and claimed that members were being held against their will. As a result, Leo Ryan, a Congressman, came to inspect Jonestown in November 1978. At first, the visit went well, but later, several Temple members decided that they wanted to leave Jonestown with the visitors. Jones' response was drastic. While Ryan and the others were waiting to leave at the local airstrip, some of the Temple's security guards arrived and started shooting. Congressman Ryan and four others, including three members of the press, were killed. Fearing retribution, the cult members decided to commit group suicide—914 died, 638 adults and 276 children. Many drank a lethal cyanide concoction. Others appeared to have been murdered by poisonous injection. Some were shot. A few fled into the jungle and survived. The Guyanese coroner said that hundreds of bodies showed needle marks, indicating foul play.

The People's Temple organization did not survive the mass suicide/murder in Guyana. The Loma-Prieta earthquake of 1989 destroyed their former headquarters building in San Francisco.

Affidavit of Deborah Layton Blakey
(See *Seductive Poison: A Jonestown Survivor's Story of Life and Death in the Peoples Temple*, Doubleday,1998)

Excerpt from "The threat and possibility of mass suicide by members of the People's Temple," June 15, 1978, By Deborah Layton Blakey.

"I arrived in Guyana in December 1977. I spent a week in Georgetown and then, pursuant to orders, traveled to Jonestown. Conditions at Jonestown were even worse than I had feared they would be. The settlement was swarming with armed guards. No one was permitted to leave unless on a special assignment and these assignments were given only to the most trusted. We were allowed to associate with Guyanese people only while on a "mission." The vast majority of the Temple members were required to work in the fields from 7 a.m. to 6 p.m. six days per week and on Sunday from 7 a.m. to 2 p.m. We were allowed one hour for lunch. Most of this hour was spent walking back to lunch and standing in line for our food. Taking any other breaks during the workday was severely frowned upon.

"The food was woefully inadequate. There was rice for breakfast, rice-water soup for lunch, and rice and beans for dinner. On Sunday, we each received an egg and a cookie. However, the food did improve markedly on the few occasions when there were outside visitors. In contrast, Rev. Jones, claiming problems with his blood sugar, dined separately and ate meat regularly. He had his own refrigerator which was stocked with food. The two women with whom he resided, Maria Katsaris and Carolyn Layton, and the two small boys who lived with him, Kimo Prokes and John Stoen, dined with the membership. However, they were in much better physical shape than everyone else since they were also allowed to eat the food in Rev. Jones' refrigerator.

"In February 1978, conditions had become so bad that half of Jonestown was ill with severe diarrhea and high fevers. I was seriously ill for two weeks. Like most of the other sick people, I was not given any nourishing foods to help recover. I was given water and a tea drink until I was well enough to return to the basic rice and beans diet. As the former financial secretary, I was aware that the Temple received over $65,000 in Social Security checks per month. It made me angry to see that only a fraction of the income of the senior citizens in the care of the Temple was being used for their benefit. Some of the money was being used to build a settlement that would earn Rev. Jones the place in history with which he was so obsessed. The balance was being held in "reserve". Although I felt terrible about what was happening, I was afraid to say anything because I knew that anyone with a differing opinion gained the wrath of Jones and other members."

4.3.3 Branch Davidians

The Branch Davidian cult was formed in 1942 by Victor Houteff, as a breakaway group from the Seventh-Day-Adventist Church. The cult was originally called the Davidian Seventh-Day-Adventists, because it was based on the imminent Second Coming of Jesus, to establish the Kingdom of David. (This is one of the cornerstones of the Seventh-Day-Adventist Church doctrine). The members believed that Jesus would come to Earth again only after the purification of a suitable number of Christians. The Davidians believed that they were the chosen ones to be purified, and that only they would survive Armageddon. The cult was a small one, but is worth describing because of its typical autocratic setup, because of its withdrawal to a restricted compound near Waco, Texas, and especially because of its end, involving unnecessarily violent action by federal law enforcement agents.

In the 1980s, there was a power struggle between the hereditary leader of the group, George Roden, and a newcomer called Vernon Howell, who later named himself David Koresh, after the Jewish King David and the Babylonian King Cyrus.

Koresh became leader when Rodin was committed to a mental asylum after killing a friend. Koresh quickly assumed command, and informed his followers that all but he and his "spiritual wives" must become celibate. He then took many of the women (and, perhaps, underage females) as wives and fathered several children by them. The cult believed that the "lamb" of God quoted in Revelation 5:2 was not Jesus Christ, as most Christians believe, but was their leader, David Koresh.

The Waco compound, with about 130 residents, apparently contained illegal weapons. Also, the authorities believed that children were being abused. The U.S. Bureau of Alcohol, Tobacco, and Firearms stormed the compound in 1993, when Koresh refused to accept a search warrant, but were repelled with some deaths on both sides. Subsequently the FBI took over, and eventually attacked, causing the eventual death of about eighty Branch Davidians, partly by fires of unknown origin. During this struggle, the Davidians believed that it was the Battle of Armageddon. Some of the consultants hired by the FBI, including psychologists and anticult experts, were so unaware of the dynamics of doomsday cults and of the Branch Davidian beliefs and practices that they advised the FBI to take aggressive action, assuring them that the possibility of resistance and of mass suicide was low. A nonviolent resolution was possible, since Koresh promised to surrender if he was given time to write a document explaining the seven seals of Revelation. The final attack started five days later, while he was writing the book. About 250 surviving Branch Davidian members and relatives later sued the federal government. They claimed that during the assault on the Waco compound, federal agents fired tear gas canisters, which caught fire and burned down the entire compound, killing many of the Davidians.

Two small Davidian groups remained in the year 2004. One was anti-Koresh and the other believed that David Koresh would return and lead them to the promised land. Many members are reconciled to the eventual demise of the cult, as old members die off and new ones are not found. The moral of this story is that cult groups like the Branch Davidians should be carefully monitored, but that violent action against them is generally unwarranted, as long as the general public is not threatened.

4.3.4 Homicides directed against the public:

The Family (Charles Manson)

In 1967, after spending most of his adult life in prison for minor crimes, Charles Milles Manson (born in 1934) became the leader of a small group—thirty to one hundred people—known as "The Family," which had several characteristics of the classic cult. His followers were misfits seeking affection and support. They became fanatically loyal to Manson, through his personal charisma, and his clever utilization of sex, drugs, and pseudoreligious dogma. He implied to them that he was Jesus Christ reborn, and they apparently believed him. Inspired by the Beatles' song "Helter Skelter" and other songs from the White Album, Manson predicted an impending racial and nuclear war—which he called Helter Skelter—based on the biblical prophecy of Armageddon in the Book of Revelation.

In 1969, he told his followers that it was time to start "Helter Skelter," which he believed he could incite by killing prominent white people and leaving clues which implicated the Black Panthers. His followers killed seven people in the wealthy Beverly Hills section of Los Angeles, California, including the movie actress Sharon Tate, who was eight months pregnant. The murder case and subsequent trial were major news stories throughout the world because of the high profile victims, the brutality of the killings, and the unique backgrounds of the people accused of killing them. Manson and several of his followers were found guilty of murder in January 1971. In 2005, he was still in prison.

Aum Shinrikyo Cult

The Aum Shinrikyo cult, also known as Aum Supreme Truth and later as Aleph, was a Japanese religious group which mixed

Buddhist and Hindu beliefs. Aum is Sanskrit for the "powers of destruction and creation in the universe," and Shinrikyo means the "teaching of the supreme truth." As the group's name suggests, the goal was to teach the truth about the creation and destruction of the universe. The cult was founded by Shoko Asahara in 1986. The movement was granted official "religious group" status by the Japanese government in 1987. It attracted so many graduates from Japan's elite universities that it was soon dubbed a "religion for the elite." Asahara engaged in lecture tours, during which he explained his views on religion, society, and life, and answered questions with reportedly unusual wit. The usual problems with cults occurred, such as the mandatory renunciation of family and the appropriation of all the wealth of new members. As the cult became more powerful and wealthy, it had aspirations of political power. When that goal became hopeless, the cult turned to destructive acts, presumably in self-fulfillment of its predictions of Armageddon. In 1990, the cult released botulinum toxin from a vehicle driving around the Diet and other government buildings in central Tokyo. In 1993, cult members released anthrax by spraying it from an office building, and from a truck near the Imperial Palace. These attacks, presumably in response to legal actions against the cult, caused considerable illness and havoc, but no deaths. The authorities apparently suspected the cult, but were unable to prevent further attacks.

In 1995, the cult carried out a massive attack on the Tokyo subway system, by releasing sarin gas simultaneously on several subway trains. Twelve subway riders were killed and thousands were injured in the attack. Shoko Asahara and a number of senior Aum Shinrikyo officials were arrested and convicted of planning the attack. The cult still operates in Japan, but has changed its doctrine. Religious texts related to controversial Vajrayana Buddhist doctrines that authorities claimed were "justifying murder" were removed. The group apologized to the victims of the sarin gas attack and established a special compensations fund. In 1995, the group was reported as having nine thousand members in Japan, and as many as forty thousand worldwide. As of 2004, Aum Shinrikyo-Aleph membership was estimated at 1,500 to 2,000 persons.

4.4 Conclusions

Because of the desires of humans for a religious belief and for acceptance by a peer group, and because of certain weaknesses of existing religious faiths, new cults will always appear. The cult of today could be the religion of tomorrow. Some cults have had long lives, but almost all eventually succumb. Central or local governments can control some cult abuses, but cannot control every aspect of each person's life. The state can only prevent gross abuses of human rights. Thus, when a cult requires its followers to obey certain unlawful commands, for example, that underage females be wedded to the person of the cult leader's choice, the community must intervene to prevent such abuses. But often the day-to-day activities of such cult groups are not known. Often, the cult sets up its own residential compound, as in the case of the Branch Davidians of Waco, Texas. The control of such religious groups is all but impossible.

Society finds cults objectionable for several reasons:

1. Brainwashing to recruit new members.
2. Forcing converts to forsake their families and friends.
3. Forcing converts to sign over their wealth.
4. Forcing members to live in strict obedience to the cult leader.
5. Allowing members no individual freedom.
6. Sexual misconduct and perversion by the leaders.
7. Greed and selfishness of the leaders.
8. Armageddon ideas, leading to mass suicide
9. Mistreatment of children, including depriving them of education.

These objections all have some basis in fact, and indeed some of them were true for those cults that later developed into major religions, such as Christianity, Islam and Buddhism.

In recent history, it has been suggested that the present prejudice against cults, especially in regard to their "brainwashing" method of getting new converts, presents a considerable threat to evangelical Christianity. For example, in his book, *Battle for the Mind: A Physiology of Conversion and Brainwashing* (1957), William Sargant treated evangelical conversion as a classic example of brainwashing. More recently, this argument has been developed by Flo Conway and Jim Siegelman in their book *Snapping: America's Epidemic of Sudden Personality Change* (1995), where the conversion process of born-again Christians is compared to that of groups like the Moonies. Such books, and stories in the media about brainwashing, led to considerable pressure on governments in the USA, Canada, Britain, and Germany for anti-conversion laws. Nevertheless, judging by the enormous growth in Evangelical and Pentecostal Churches in recent years, it seems that these efforts were inconsequential. In China, the growth of Christian-based cults and sects is exploding, with millions of new converts. The Chinese regime has tried to suppress some cults and sects, notably the important Buddhist-Taoist movement called Falun Gong. It seems that the cult movement is one that will remain strong in the foreseeable future.

5

POWER

God may be subtle, but He isn't plain mean.
—Albert Einstein

*He who merely knows right principles is not equal to him who
loves them.*—Confucius

5.1 Overview

As cults become sects and religions, they inevitably exert various forms of power on their followers. The benevolent management of this power has always been a major challenge to religion. The abuse of power comes in many forms.

1. **Spiritual power.** "Our God is better than your God. Therefore we are better (more pious) than you infidels. Our God demands that you obey him—that is, obey his representatives on Earth, our clerics."
2. **Territorial or doctrinal power.** "Our sect (religion or doctrine) is better than any other, so our will should be imposed on everyone, by military force if necessary."
3. **Intellectual and Cultural Power.** "Our religion will teach you how to be a better person, but first you have to follow certain rules, which you will learn in our churches and schools." (See also Chapter 6. Dogma.)

---

4. **Sexual Power.** "Men are better than women, and have been told by God that they must exert firm control over women." (See Chapters 7 and 8.)
5. **Personal Power.** "As your spiritual leader, I am favored by God, and should receive special advantages, including adulation and unlimited wealth." (See also Chapter 4. Cults.)

One can assume that religious leaders have the responsibility to use their power to direct people toward benevolent goals, but often this power has been diverted toward malevolent purposes. This frequent deviation from the religious ideals of humility and benevolence can be explained, at least partly, by the human trait (or instinct) of aggression, which, in turn, can lead to fanaticism. Human aggression arises from only two causes, genetic and environmental. Konrad Lorenz, in his important research on the nature of man, found that aggressive behavior was a basic trait of humans, caused by their instinct for survival (see his book, *On Aggression*). In order to survive, they found it necessary to defend their territory aggressively against wild animals and other humans, and the genes for this behavior were inherited. Although this analysis of human aggressive qualities has now been questioned by many modern psychologists and anthropologists, the concept is an important one, and not lightly dismissed. It is easy to understand that the instinct for survival can result in the desire to control one's environment, and ultimately, lead to the aggressive quest for power over groups of people and nations. Not only this "territorial" power, but also sexual power, cultural power, and personal power achieved through wealth, have arisen in religious scandals.

Environmental causes of aggression are well known. An aggressive parent teaches his child to behave the same way. Similarly, in order to reach the pinnacle of his profession, any leader, including a religious leader, is often required to lobby aggressively for peer support. Therefore, it is natural for both environmental and genetic reasons, that some religious leaders developed aggressive patterns and abused their power. This problem is exacerbated in **organized** religion, rather than in the individual practice of religious rites and philosophies. Whereas fanaticism is the vehicle by which power is executed, spirituality is the peaceful way to avoid such abuses.

Religions have evolved continuously through the ages, both to promote the benefits of power, and to overcome the abuses of power. The coalescing of sects into powerful, monolithic Churches has benefited society by the unification of moral codes, the development of cohesive family and community life, and the efficient dispensing of charity. Conversely, the splintering of Churches and the creation of new sects—occurring because of religious abuses, rigid dogma, and excessive control—have benefited mankind by creating a freer, more tolerant, and more forgiving populace. For example, the enlightened philosophy of Buddhism arose because of dissatisfaction with the rigid power-structure and excessive rites of Hinduism. As a result of the rise of Buddhism, Hinduism recreated itself into a more humanistic religion. Protestantism was initiated to combat personal corruption and the abuse of sacramental power in Catholicism. This religious revival contributed to the Age of Enlightenment, and thus to the eventual preeminence of the modern Western world. In every religion, new sects are continuously being created in response to real or perceived flaws in doctrine or the abuse of power.

How can abuses of religious power be overcome? One answer lies in the triumph of spirituality over fanaticism. The true meaning of religion is spiritual communion with God. The bane of religion is corruption caused by the fanatic lust for power. The ultimate answer must lie in better education. Religions controlled education until about two hundred years ago, and still do in parts of the Muslim world. Religious schools teach intolerance of other faiths, and thus of different human ideals and aspirations. In advanced nations, the education of young minds is not left to the Churches, because people realize that religious education is too rigid. However, there is still a strong influence of Christian dogma in the curricula of Western schools. The secularization of education has been an important part of modern progress, and has undoubtedly contributed greatly to the development of scientific knowledge and, thereby, to the improvement of human welfare. Mandatory inclusion of classes about world religions in both religious and secular schools would improve worldwide religious tolerance, reduce the influence of rigid religious dogma, and combat fanaticism.

5.2 Spiritual Power

5.2.1 The Fear of God

Since the ancient times of religion, in which holy men or Shamans exercised enormous power over the minds of their subjects, the fear of mysterious spirits, and ultimately of a vengeful God, dominated religion. The basic reason for this fear was a lack of knowledge about the forces of nature, so that these forces were attributed to various powerful gods. Shamans exploited this ignorance and fear of nature to further their own power. To guarantee a bountiful harvest, humans had to appease and please the gods by suitable ceremonies, sometimes including animal and human sacrifice.

Gradually, the number of rituals and sacrifices increased until they became a great burden for humans. This burden was likely a major cause of the development of alternate religions. An early example was the emergence of Christianity in the Jewish areas of the Middle East, which may have been due to the excessive control of Judaism over the spiritual lives of Jews, reflected in excessive ritual. Similarly, the Protestant Reformation was a reaction against the inordinate use of Roman Catholic sacraments, which were considered necessary for the spiritual lives of Christians.

Excessive spiritual control may even lead to the demise of an entire people. In the Easter Islands, the obsession to erect giant statues of the gods became the most important aspect of their culture. The result was that the islands were deforested in the competition to pursue this massive project, and the whole civilization collapsed (see *Collapse: How Societies Choose to Fail or Succeed* by Jared Diamond). There are many other examples of the negative effects of spiritual power, such as the practice of human sacrifice, common in Central America, and the use in Sufism of hallucinatory drugs, such as hashish, to create a trancelike state in worshipers, for example, the "whirling dervishes."

5.2.2 Colonization

In the centuries from 1500-1900, the Christian nations of Europe engaged in a frenzy of competitive expansion into North and South America, Africa, Asia, and Australia. The resulting catastrophic enslavement and annihilation of aboriginal peoples by the colonial powers has been documented many times. The role of the Christian Church in this disaster was important, since the forcible replacement of native spirituality and religions with Christian concepts contributed to the breakdown of the indigenous cultures. The native populations in many of these areas were all but eliminated by the effects of war, enslavement and disease. The total loss of life caused by colonization is estimated at between thirty million and one hundred million persons in North and South America alone. (See *Rivers of Blood, Rivers of Gold: Europe's Conquest of Indigenous Peoples*, by Mark Cocker, and *Guns, Germs and Steel: The Fates of Human Societies*, by Jared Diamond.) Although the primary cause of the deaths was disease brought to these lands by the colonialists, the effects of cruel treatment and enslavement must have played an important role in natives' mortality from the new diseases, by weakening their natural resistance through starvation and overwork. Religious leaders share in the responsibility for this catastrophe.

The purposes of this colonization were to achieve power through exploitation of the riches of these lands, to promote trade and, as a sort of bonus, to convert the "heathen" of these lands to Christianity. The first two of these goals were perfectly understandable and logical goals of politicians. The third was likewise a reasonable goal of Christianity. However, it was the duty of the religious leaders to observe their own moral codes, and not to treat the natives of the subjugated lands as inferior human beings. The Church should have controlled the excesses and brutality of the colonists, and resisted the enslavement of the native peoples. There were, it is true, a few religious leaders who objected to the depravity of the colonists. Notably, Father Bartolome de Las Casas of Spain wrote many articles and a book (*A Short Account of the Destruction of the Indies*, Penguin Classics, 1992) about the horrible cruelty of the Spanish occupation of the West Indies. He even tried judicially to prevent further atrocities, but, sadly, these efforts were in vain. Now, of course, it is politically correct to admire the "noble savage," and to respect his customs and religion. Humans have indeed become more tolerant in the interim.

The Catholic Church all but destroyed the native spiritual heritage by systematically eliminating the literature and religious symbols of the ancient cultures of Central and South America. The friars and priests were so zealous in their pursuit of converts that they deemed it necessary to destroy virtually all native religious temples, artifacts and literature. For example, in 1562, Friar Diego de Landa organized the public burning of thousands of manuscripts at the main square of Mani in Yucatan Province. He wrote, "We found great numbers of books, but as they contained nothing but superstitions and falsehoods of the devil, we burned them all, which the natives took most grievously, and which gave them great pain." (See his book, *Yucatan Before and After the Conquest*.) Of the many thousands of codices and scrolls that described the native religions, history and culture in that region, less than two dozen survived (see *Fingerprints of the Gods*, by Graham Hancock). Juan de Zumarraga, Bishop of Mexico, boasted that he had destroyed twenty thousand idols and five hundred Indian temples. Fortunately, a few knowledgeable and humane friars belatedly sought to preserve some of the ancient native culture. One of the most noted of these was Bernardino de Sahagun, a Franciscan Friar and linguist who collected considerable information about the history, religion and anthropology of ancient Mexico. (See *Mysteries of the Mexican Pyramids*, by Peter Tompkins.)

Was Christianity "better" than the native religions? When Christopher Columbus landed on the Caribbean Island of Hispaniola (now shared by Haiti and the Dominican Republic) in 1492, he noted with amazement that the Arawak natives (now extinct) were full of love and generosity. He sent a letter to his sponsors, King Ferdinand and Queen Isabella of Spain, saying " . . . they are so guileless and so generous with all that they possess, that no one would believe it who has not seen it. Of anything they have, if they are asked for it, they never say no, on the contrary they invite the person to share it and display as much love as if they would give their hearts . . ." (*Wild Majesty: Encounters with Caribs from Columbus to the Present Day*, P. Hulme and N. Whitehead, Oxford, 1992). This is an attitude that Jesus Christ himself would praise. Why would the missionaries think that their religion provided a superior spiritual base and moral code to that of the natives? Because they were brainwashed into believing that only their God and religion could save souls.

5.3. Territorial or Doctrinal Power

Paradoxically, the most dogmatic and warlike ecclesiastics have been monotheists, although the concept of a single, all-powerful God, common to all mankind, should preclude intolerant attitudes toward other religions. However, the desire of religious leaders for power convinced them that their version of the "will of God" demanded that they convert and conquer "infidels." The resultant religious wars have had a significant impact on history, perhaps even more than the more deadly and far-reaching major wars of conquest, such as the First and Second World Wars, and the remarkable military feats of the Mongols and of Alexander the Great. Probably the most successful religious war of all was the lightning conquest of most of the Near East and North Africa, and some of Western Europe by the Muslims in the years following the revelations of Muhammad in 622. Religious wars were waged not only against the "infidels," as were the great Islamic invasions of the seventh century and the Crusades of the twelfth and thirteenth centuries, but also against people of similar religion. For example, the Christian crusade against the Cathars in Southern France and Northern Italy, and the Thirty Years War in Europe.

5.3.1. Intrareligious strife

It seems inevitable that the thirst for ecclesiastical power leads to schisms in major religions. Hinduism dominated the religious experience of India for about a thousand years after the arrival of the Indo-Aryan culture around 1500 BCE, until about 550 BCE, when the abuses and the overly rigid and ritualistic form of Hinduism caused widespread discontent. The result was the formation of many religious splinter groups. Buddhism, a radically new philosophical form of Hinduism, emerged and quickly became a powerful alternative to Hinduism. After that, a power struggle persisted for more than one thousand years. During that period, Hinduism adopted sufficient reforms that it again became the dominant religion of India in the twelfth century. During this time, Hinduism was in competition also with Islam.

Buddhism itself spread to many Asian states, and around the first century of the Christian era split into two major factions, the older **Theravada**, or Way of the Elders and the newer **Mahayana**, or Followers of the Greater Vehicle of Salvation. Theravada, also disparagingly called Hinanyana (Followers of the Lesser Vehicle of Salvation) by the upstart Mahayana, emphasized wisdom. It appealed to intellectuals and to those who were willing to withdraw from a normal life into one of isolation and meditation. It is common in Sri Lanka, Myanmar, Thailand and Indonesia. Mahayana is a more liberal form of Buddhism that emphasizes compassion, and it dominated in China, Japan, Tibet and Mongolia. As is common in religions, these different denominations resulted from different interpretations of the teachings of the prophet. In contrast to the power struggles in other major religions, it appears that the Buddhists split rather amicably, without major loss of life.

In Christianity, spiritual, cultural and hierarchal splits have occurred since its inception. Initially, there was a struggle for power among the Jewish Christians, the Gnostics and the Pauline Christians. Within two hundred years, the Pauline Christians prevailed, giving the world the present version of Christianity, in which Jesus Christ became God. The first major schism in established Christianity occurred in 1054, when the Eastern Orthodox Church separated from the Roman Catholic Church, largely because of ideological differences, including the primacy of the Pope, the question of the worship of idols, and the dogma of the Holy Trinity. This split became irreconcilable after the slaughter of Constantinople's Christians by the Western Christians during the Fourth Crusade.

The next major schism in Christianity occurred with the Reformation of the sixteenth century, initiated by Luther and Calvin. It was caused largely by the corruption of high Roman Catholic officials, including Popes, especially highlighted by the unscrupulous practice of the Church in utilizing holy sacraments and "indulgences" for monetary purposes. The Church became very wealthy from these two methods of tithing. At least seven different sacraments were designated as essential for a pious Catholic, and each involved payments to the Church. They became a considerable burden for the average citizen, even for those of considerable means, such as the middle-class artisans and knights. The spark that lit the flame of revolt was the practice of indulgences, which permitted the forgiveness of sins by suitable payments to the Church. In 1517, Martin Luther, a Catholic priest in Germany, became so enraged about these excesses that he published and posted on his Wittenburg church door his famous ninety-five proclamations criticizing the papacy. In a surprisingly short time, this criticism led to the creation of the Lutheran Church. Similarly, John Calvin, a law and theology student in France, fought for reform in the 1530s. His Protestant movement was established in Geneva, Switzerland, and became the model for the Reformed Church, which is the basis of the modern state churches of the Netherlands and Scotland, as well as reformist churches in Germany and North America. About the same time, the English Anglican Church broke away from the Catholic Church, largely because of a power conflict concerning papal authority over the English ecclesiastics. Other internal power struggles occurred in Christianity, notably the efforts of the Anabaptists and Cathars to create somewhat modified versions of Christianity. These efforts were met by violent resistance and persecution.

In Islam, very soon after this new religion swept through the Mediterranean region in the seventh century, a major split occurred over the succession of power. The Sunnis, who form the major part of Islam today, wanted the supreme leader to be decided by a religious council, whereas the Shiites wanted the leader to be a direct descendant of Muhammad. The strife caused by this power struggle persists today. Muslims have slaughtered each other during much of the intervening time because of this difference.

I. Conquest of the Cathars

By the beginning of the eleventh century, the Roman Catholic Church had become a powerful establishment, owning vast lands and riches. The Church had to compete not only with powerful feudal barons and kings, but also with religious sects that arose because of fundamental religious differences. The Cathars were one of these sects.

The Albigensians or Cathars formed a dualist religious sect that began around the year 1000. Its origin was much more ancient, and stemmed from the Baltic, so that its followers were also called Bougres (Bulgarians). They were called Albigensians because one group was centered about the Southern French town of Albi. Later they became known as the Cathars, from the French word for "pure." The concept of dualism is ancient, arising from the Zoroastrians in Persia, millennia before the Christian time, and continuing through the Gnostics and Manichaeans of the early centuries of the Christian era. Dualism means that there are two Gods, a "good" God that created the spiritual world, and a "bad" God that created the evil, material world. Cathars were persecuted or "disciplined" by the Church, but persisted and grew remarkably over the next two centuries, until they were decimated by a Catholic crusade and then gradually eliminated by the inquisition. In fact, their main legacy was being the major cause of the Inquisition, which flourished long after they were gone. Their ascent to a position of religious dominance in Southern France and Northern Italy, in the face of extremely strong opposition and persecution by the Catholic Church, was even more remarkable because of the extreme asceticism of their beliefs.

The Cathars believed that all matter was evil, but that the human heart or spirit was the temple through which God should be worshiped. This radical idea (for that time) was dangerous for the preservation of the powerful Catholic hierarchy, for it meant that the vast network of churches, cathedrals, and monasteries belonging to the Church were superfluous. Like other Christian sects of that time, the Cathars were quite ascetic. They detested the corruption and greed of the Catholic hierarchy. In the less extreme faction of Cathars ("believers"), the evil God was a fallen angel, like the Christian devil, but in the extreme faction ("the perfect"), the good God manifested itself only in the soul of each individual, and the bad God created the universe, so that all matter was evil. The bulk of the Cathars were "believers," who did not attain the purity of the "perfect" Cathars. The "perfect" believed that any form of food resulting from "coition," or mating, was forbidden. Thus they were strict vegetarians. Sexual intercourse was forbidden, as it led to creation of more evil matter. They devoted themselves to meditation—in this category were their bishops and deacons. The "perfect" were spiritually baptized in the elaborate "consolamentum," and the "believers" could receive this sacrament just before death. The Cathars rewrote the biblical story; the Old Testament was largely rejected, and the New Testament was revised—Jesus was merely an angel who came to Earth to point the way to salvation via his (illusory) suffering and death.

The Cathars were treated as heretics from 1012. The first execution of Cathars as heretics occurred in Toulouse in 1022, but a major crusade against them took place only about two hundred years later, when their power in southern France, under the protection of several feudal lords around Toulouse, became too great. In effect, a civil war took place between the barons of northern France and those of the South.

The Cathar sect grew most rapidly from 1140-1170, following the failure of the Gregorian reform of the Catholic Church. Many common people, including merchants, artisans, lower clergy and poorer knights, who could not afford the expenses of the many sacraments required by the Church, joined religious sects like the Cathars and the Waldenses[8]. The Cathars established an organized church, with a hierarchy, a liturgy and a system of doctrine. In about 1149, the first bishop appeared in the North of France, and others soon were established in Albi and Lombardy. Following the visit of the Bogomil bishop, Nicetas, to Lombardy and southern France in 1167, which enhanced the prestige of the Cathars, several Cathar bishoprics were created, four in the south of France and six in Northern Italy. The Cathars in southern France adopted the more radical dualism, in which Satan, the creator of the Earth, was an independent deity, whereas those in Italy were split between the radical approach and the more moderate one, in which Satan was merely a fallen angel, and God created the universe. Both factions agreed that all matter was evil, and man must free himself from this evil environment.

In 1184, largely as a result of the astonishingly rapid growth of the Cathars, the Catholic Church, personified by Pope Lucius III and Emperor Frederick I Barbarossa, issued a decree *ad abolendum*, which established a procedure for trial of various heretics by the church, followed by punishment by the secular authorities. Punishment could mean confiscation of property,

---

[8]　The Waldenses were one of the few sects of the period that have survived to the present day. The movement was founded in Southern France at the end of the twelfth century by the layman, Valdes (also called Peter Waldo). Their doctrine was poverty and repentance, and they repudiated purgatory, pilgrimages, the holiness of the church, and secular law courts. The movement spread rapidly through France, Spain, Italy, Germany, and even Poland. The Waldenses, being laymen, as well as heretical, were persecuted severely by the Catholic Church. For example, in 1211, eighty were burned at the stake in Strasbourg. The movement had a revival in the sixteenth century, being transformed from a medieval sect into a Protestant church, centered around the Cottian Alps along the French-Italian border. It was not until 1848 that they received full civil rights. In the late nineteenth century, many Waldenses emigrated to South America and The United States of America.

exile, or death. For unrepentant heretics, death was commonly by burning. Of all the sects denounced in this decree, only the Waldenses survive today.

Pope Innocent III (1198-1216) tried to persuade the heretics to convert, But when the Papal envoy, Peter de Castelnau, was murdered in 1208 while on a mission to Raymond VI, count of Toulouse, the Pope declared a Crusade against the Cathars. A considerable army led by the barons of the North attacked and ravaged Toulouse, slaughtering Catholics and Cathars indiscriminately. The final victory of the crusade was the capture and destruction of the fortress of Montsegur near the Pyrenees in 1244. After that, organized resistance ceased, and the Inquisition gradually stamped out the last of the Cathars early in the fifteenth century.

The accounts of inquisitors may represent the best description of the Cathars' beliefs, although they are, of course, biased. One description, by Bernard Gui, quoted in the Medieval Sourcebook, referred to the Cathars or Albigensians, as follows: "Of baptism, they assert that the water is material and corruptible and is therefore the creation of the evil power, and cannot sanctify the soul, but that the churchmen sell this water out of avarice, just as they sell earth for the burial of the dead, and oil to the sick when they anoint them, and as they sell the confession of sins as made to the priests. Hence they claim that confession made to the priests of the Roman Church is useless, and that, since the priests may be sinners, they cannot loose nor bind, and, being unclean in themselves, cannot make others clean. They assert, moreover, that the cross of Christ should not be adored or venerated, because, as they urge, no one would venerate or adore the gallows upon which a father, relative, or friend had been hung. They urge, further, that they who adore the cross ought, for similar reasons, to worship all thorns and lances, because as Christ's body was on the cross during the passion, so was the crown of thorns on his head and the soldier's lance in his side. They proclaim many other scandalous things in regard to the sacraments. Moreover they read from the Gospels and the Epistles in the vulgar tongue, applying and expounding them in their favor and against the condition of the Roman Church in a manner which it would take too long to describe in detail; but all that relates to this subject may be read more fully in the books they have written and infected, and may be learned from the confessions of such of their followers as have been converted." (from *The Inquisitor's Manual of Bernard Gui*, early fourteenth century, translated by J. H. Robinson in *Readings in European History*).

The sad and violent ending of the Cathar movement is a good example of how spirituality succumbs to rigid dogmatism and fanatic desire for power. The first lesson to be learned is that drastic changes in religion, as in all human endeavors, are difficult to achieve. The second lesson is that spiritual ideas, taken to the extreme, so that they contradict common sense, lead to disaster. The Cathars had a good concept, that the Church should become more spiritual and less greedy. They carried their idea to the extreme, however, by labeling all matter as corrupt, and even condemning sexual intercourse. They became fanatic in their spirituality. In contrast, the Franciscan order, founded by St. Francis, preached a more loving scripture, in which the World was good and joyful, and this ultimately appealed more to the masses.

II. The Thirty Years War (1618-1648)

The Thirty Years War was basically a conflict between Catholics and Protestants in central Europe, although it also involved struggles for power among the kings and dukes of Austria, Germany, Sweden, Denmark, France, Spain, the Netherlands and Britain. The seeds of this disastrous war lay in the reformist movements of Luther and Calvin. The success of the Reformation meant that many of the Catholic dioceses and land were taken over by Protestants. This process was opposed by the Jesuit counter-reformation. By the Peace of Augsburg in 1555, the status quo existing in 1552 between the Catholic and Lutheran boundaries was formalized. Neither side was satisfied by this agreement, especially the Lutherans, as those boundaries did not fairly represent Lutheran-controlled areas. The peace did not include any rights for the Calvinists. It prohibited any bishopric from becoming Lutheran, even if the overwhelming majority of its citizens wished it. Moreover, it did not allow for any judicial settling of disputes, or any method of enforcement of the provisions. The result was that Catholic sovereignty over a territory prevented local populations from appointing Protestant bishops or clergy. For example, Bavarian princes, notably Maximilian I, maintained control of the archbishopric of Cologne over the entire period from 1583-1761. The city was not permitted to become Protestant in 1583 when the people as well as their leader, archbishop Gebhard, who had converted to Protestantism, wished it. Gebhard was excommunicated and deposed by force.

As in most wars, political and social aspects were also important. Europe in the early seventeenth century had evolved into a collection of kings, princes, and dukes who controlled large territories. The major powers were the Holy Roman Empire, centered in Austria, and the Kingdom of Spain, which extended to Northern Italy and the Netherlands. The Protestant part of the Netherlands was in the process of breaking away from Spanish sovereignty, the Scandinavian states of Denmark and Sweden were struggling for control of the Baltic ports, and Bavaria, though Catholic, wanted to maintain its independence from the Empire. In Germany, the North was Protestant, and the South was Catholic. Germany was the only country where the Reformation caused a permanent schism into three religious denominations, Catholic, Lutheran and Calvinist. Therefore, it was inevitable that Germany became the major battlefield for this conflict. France was in a difficult position, having little power and being surrounded by the Catholic Habsburg realms of Spain and Bohemia-Austria-Hungary, under the Holy Roman Emperor. Spain also controlled parts of Northern Italy, and was involved in a civil war to retain its Dutch possessions. The Emperor Ferdinand opposed the ascendancy of Lutheran-controlled areas, not only for religious reasons, but also because Lutheran princes tended toward independence from central control. The major result of the thirty Years War was that a loose confederation of states prevailed, rather than the centrally controlled Holy Roman Empire. By unreasonably trying to retain power over Protestant regions, the Roman Catholic Church lost an enormous amount of both influence and good will.

An important political and economic aspect of the Thirty Years War was that the era of the great city-states of Germany (as well as Italy), such as Hamburg, Bremen, Danzig, Nuernberg, Frankfurt, and Augsburg was ending, as territorial princes assumed control. The downfall of the independent Northern German cities, which were loosely united as the Hanseatic League, was hastened by the Russian destruction of Novgorod (1570), the Spanish sacking of Antwerp (1585) and the British (in the reign of Elizabeth I) closing of the London Steelworks (1598). The rising independence of the Dutch naval cities from the Spanish yoke provided severe competition in trading. The Southern German cities, which were very strong in banking, had a series of bankruptcies. The severe inflation from 1619-23, exacerbated by the war and by officially sanctioned counterfeiters, sealed the fate of the great banking towns like Frankfurt and Augsburg. As an example of the plight of other German cities, Leipzig went bankrupt in 1625, was attacked in 1631, 1632, 1633, 1637 and 1642, experienced the major battles of Breitenfeld in 1631 and 1642, as well as the battle of Luetzen in 1632, and was occupied by the Swedes from 1642-50. Nevertheless, the annual Leipzig Fair was established as a center of European trade during those difficult times.

The major Catholic leaders of the conflict were Ferdinand II of Austria (the Habsburg Holy Roman Emperor), his cousin, King Philip IV of Spain, and the able Maximilian of Bavaria. They were opposed by the leaders of Denmark, Holland, France, Sweden, and Northern Germany. Much of the war was fought in Germany, with the Catholic South opposed by the Protestant North. Even today, Germany is split North from South along religious lines. Since many of the armies were mercenary, and were not adequately financed by their sponsoring powers, the soldiers had to survive by looting the countryside. After thirty years of war and pillaging, Germany was so ravaged that it was not again a major power for 150 years.

The war consumed most of central Europe. The Protestant princes formed a union that was opposed by the Catholic

League. Major Catholic generals were Tilly of Bavaria, Duke Wallenstein of Friedland, Spinola of Spain, and Count Buquoi of Austria. The first important leader of the Protestants was the mercenary general Ernst von Mansfeld, who almost overthrew Emperor Ferdinand in the early stages of the War, before the Bavarian and Spanish armies defeated him near the gates of Vienna in 1620. As the Protestant situation deteriorated, King Christian IV of Denmark and Gustavus Adolphus of Sweden became major combatants for the Protestant cause. At one stage, near 1628, Wallenstein's dream of a united Germany was almost realized. However, when Christian IV was forced to sign the peace of Luebeck and the Edict of Restitution of 1629, which restored 150 Northern church districts to Catholicism, the Protestants rebelled, for they realized that this meant only one religion, Catholicism, for all of Germany. The Northern Germans appealed to King Gustavus, who invaded with his well-trained and well-paid armies. Wallenstein was blamed for this turn of events and the Emperor dismissed him. The tide of battle turned quickly, and before long, Gustavus had conquered almost all of Germany, with the exception of the Catholic stronghold of Bavaria.

At this stage, in 1632 Emperor Ferdinand was forced to reinstate Wallenstein. With his brilliant organization and military skills, Wallenstein quickly assembled an army of 60,000, which Schiller in a famous play characterized as "excellent in war and in plundering, destitute of all home and national ties, and owing allegiance to its general alone." Wallenstein and Gustavus fought more or less to a standstill, until Gustavus was killed in a huge indecisive battle at Luetzen in late 1632. At this stage, Richelieu of France entered the fray. He feared the power of Spain, and supported freedom of religion in order to suppress the central power of Vienna. In 1633, Wallenstein was successful in the North, penetrating almost to the Baltic, but, in the meantime, the Swedish army was advancing in the south, capturing Regensburg from Maximilian. Wallenstein decided that this was a good time for peace, but the Emperor, because of a renewed alliance with the Spanish, chose to dismiss Wallenstein for a second time. Wallenstein then attempted to unite with the Protestant forces for peace, but his army refused, and he was murdered in early 1634 in Eger. All efforts for peace died with him, and Germany became a plundered battlefield for the armies of Sweden, France, Spain and Austria for the next 14 years.

The armies became larger. The loss of men and the plundering of the villages of Germany, and to some extent France, became even greater. In a critical battle at Noerdlingen in 1634, General Bernhard of Sweden lost 17,000 men. Subsequently, most of the German princes dissolved their alliances with Sweden, leading to the Peace of Prague in 1635, stating that all Protestant domains as of 1627 would remain so. After that, the role of Sweden in the war was diminished, and the leadership of the Protestant cause fell to France, under the brilliant Cardinal Richelieu. He assembled an enormous French army of two hundred thousand to subdue the Spaniards and Austrians, but it was overextended by engaging the enemy on many fronts, in Alsace, Lorraine, the Rhine and Northern Italy. He attempted to form alliances with Russia and Turkey, but they proved ineffective because of internal problems and other wars of those nations. However, alliances with the United Provinces (the Netherlands), Sweden, Northern Italy and German Protestant states were more successful. The Imperialist cause was greatly weakened by the Spanish rebellions of Catalonia and Portugal in 1640. The Protestant forces gradually gained control, as the war drew to a close.

By the **Peace of Westphalia**, on October 24, 1648, Sweden received a large cash settlement, and control over Western Pomerania, Bremen and Verden. France obtained much of Lorraine and Alsace. These territories later became a source of endless conflict between Germany and France. The German princes acquired some land and became independent of the Emperor. The United Provinces of the Netherlands became independent, as did Switzerland. The major political result of the treaty was that the members of the Holy Roman Empire regained their sovereignty, including their right to form alliances, "except against the Emperor and Reich." The Emperor was to obey the decisions of the Imperial Diet, which previously was ineffective.

The Protestant leaders of the secularized bishoprics were included in the Diet with full rights. This meant that the power of Catholics, Lutherans and Calvinists became equal. The Edict of Restitution was repealed. Dissidents were allowed freedom of worship and the right to emigrate. Only in the Habsburg domains (Austria and Spain) were non-Catholics disallowed.

The Thirty Years War was a disaster for Germany, which by some accounts lost three hundred thousand men in battle and millions of civilians by disease and starvation. It has been estimated that the population of the Empire dropped from twenty-one million to about fourteen million. The power of the Holy Roman Empire was decentralized. The big winner was France, which emerged as the leading nation of Europe, replacing Spain, which lost Portugal and much of its Dutch territory. In religious matters, the Protestants gained considerable power, and freedom to worship as they chose. However, their suffering continued, especially in the Habsburg domains. In Bohemia, where they previously were the majority, Protestants were almost wiped out. Even in France the Huguenots were severely persecuted for the rest of the century.

5.3.2 Interreligious Wars

Curiously, wars between religions have not been as disastrous for humanity as wars within religions, but they still have caused much misery. Here again, it has been a question of striving for religious power, whether territorial, ethnic or doctrinal. Interreligious disagreements are still preventing an effective worldwide ecumenical movement.

I. Hindu-Muslim Conflict

The history of Hindu-Muslim strife began with the series of invasions of the Indian state of Punjab by **Mahmud** of Ghazni, king of Khorasan (eastern Afghanistan), beginning in the year 1000. The most successful early Muslim ruler was Muhammad of Ghur, who conquered most of northern India during 1175-1205. Following his rule, Qutb-ud-Din Aybak, a former slave and viceroy of Delhi, founded the so-called "slave dynasty," which controlled India until 1288. A century later, when the Muslim rule had become weak, the great Mongol leader, **Tamerlane** (Timur the Lame), invaded India and sacked Delhi in 1398. After Tamerlane withdrew, the weak Sayyid and the Lordi Muslim dynasties persisted for over a century.

In 1526, another Muslim, **Babur**, invaded India from Afghanistan, and defeated a much larger Lordi army. He was a descendant of Tamerlane on his father's side and Ghengis Khan on his mother's side. His army was of mixed blood, Mongol, Turkish, Iranian and Afghan. Babur had inherited the throne of Fergana in present-day Uzbekistan, but internal dissensions forced him to move to Kabul in Afghanistan. He founded the **Mughal** (or Mogul) empire in India. He was a cultured and compassionate ruler, who wrote poetry in Turkic and Persian. Babur did not emphasize religion, but rather his Turkic heritage.

Akbar, the grandson of Babur, was the greatest of the Mughal emperors. He ruled from 1556 to 1605. He conquered most of present India, including Punjab, Bengal, Kashmir, Sind and several kingdoms of the Deccan. He was a tolerant and wise leader, promoting trade, efficient administration and religious tolerance. He allowed new Hindu temples to be built, and personally participated in Hindu festivals such as Diwali, the festival of lights. Akbar accepted all religions and sects, encouraged remarriage of widows, discouraged child marriage and set up special market days for women. He abolished the **jizya** (poll tax) that had been imposed on non-Muslims. He established an innovative approach to taxation, based on a statistical averaging of crop yields. He assimilated Hindu leaders into the highest levels of his government. Akbar not only encouraged intermarriage between Mughal and Rajput aristocracy, but he set an example by marrying a Hindu, Maryam al-Zamani, who was the mother of his heir, Jahangir.

The Mughal Empire reached its zenith during the reign of Akbar's grandson, **Shah Jahan**, from 1628 to 1658. He married a Persian princess whom he renamed Nur Jahan (Light of the World). He is noted for promoting the arts and architecture, including the fabled **Taj Mahal**, which he built as a mausoleum for his beloved wife. Many Persian scholars, artists and poets came to the sanctuary of his court. However, he was not tolerant of other religions. He promoted mass conversion to Islam, and persecuted followers of Jainism and Sikhism. His economic policies were not productive, and military campaigns to retain and expand the Empire were very costly. It is interesting to note that the construction of the artistically triumphant, but economically excessive Taj Mahal was typical of Jahan's reign. It is comparable to the 1900 construction of the elaborate Summer Palace in Beijing by the Chinese Empress, using funds that should have been used to refurbish her navy, at a time when the European interests were threatening to take over coastal China.

After this period, the Empire gradually declined. The last important ruler, **Aurangzeb**, who ruled from 1658 to 1707, was a ruthless religious fanatic. He seized power by killing his brothers and imprisoning his father, Shah Jahan. He banned construction of new Hindu temples, destroyed several of them, and reimposed the jizya tax on non-Muslims. He banned music at court, and persecuted Sikhs. In the latter stages of his reign, provinces broke away from the Empire to form independent kingdoms. Later, Persian and Afghan armies under Nadir Shah invaded Delhi in 1739, and took many treasures, including the Peacock Throne. Again in 1756, the Mughal army was defeated by Persian armies, led by Ahmad Shah. After a century of decline, the Empire collapsed completely in 1857, when the British Empire assumed control of India.

During the struggle to free India from Great Britain in the early part of the twentieth century, **Mahatma Gandhi** was a major leader of the independence movement. His method of passive resistance proved to be fruitful. In 1931, he and the future first prime minister, **Jawaharlal Nehru**, were released from prison by the British government as part of a peace agreement. At this stage, the Muslim League, formed to protect the interests of the Muslim community, demanded special powers in the future independent government. In spite of Gandhi's pacifist policies, rioting between Hindus and Muslims occurred. But there was still hope for an Indian multicultural state, partially under the control of Britain. The Government of India Act was passed in 1935 by the British Parliament to effect this goal. The Indian National Congress, largely through the influence of Gandhi, also passed it, with serious reservations.

In 1947, shortly after the end of World War II, Prime Minister Atlee of Britain announced that India would become independent no later than June 1948, whether or not the religious factions of India could be reconciled. Lord Mountbatten, the British viceroy, believed that partition of India into separate Muslim and Hindu States was necessary to avoid a disastrous religious civil war. Consequently, Pakistan and the Union of India were created. Unfortunately, this did not prevent religious massacres and mass migration of peoples between the two new states. In just one month following the official Indian independence on August 15, 1947, more than four million refugees moved from one nation to the other, Sikhs and Hindus from Pakistan to India, and Muslims from India to Pakistan.

In the State of Bengal, relatively few problems with its partition occurred, probably because of Gandhi's influence. Religious rioting in both Calcutta and Delhi ceased when Gandhi staged hunger strikes, showing his enormous influence. He was truly a religious figure who practiced what he preached, and his stature was legendary. Consequently, his assassination in January 1948 by a Hindu fanatic exacerbated the situation. The states having the most difficulties in the partition were Punjab and Kashmir. Nearly two million Sikhs, who were anti-Islam, lived in the part of Punjab assigned to Pakistan. In Kashmir, the population was mostly Muslim, but the Maharaja was Hindu, and he decided that Kashmir should be part of India. Muslims took control of the northern part of Kashmir, resulting in a limited war between India and Pakistan. The borders partitioning Kashmir still have not been settled.

During periods of religious tolerance under Muslim rule, for example, during the reign of Akbar, India prospered, and poetry, art, philosophy, architecture, and science flourished. Under religiously fanatic leaders like Aurangzeb, who suppressed Hinduism and other religions, the Empire declined. Religious fanaticism, inspired by rigid dogma, inevitably leads to serious conflicts and deterioration of society.

II. Christian-Muslim Conflict:

Ever since the inception of Islam, there has been conflict with Christianity. Initially in the seventh century, the Muslim movement had an exceptionally fast rise to a position of world power. The Muslim hordes swept over the Christian nations of the Eastern and Southern Mediterranean in a very few years, and reached into Europe. Half of Spain and much of the Balkans were under Muslim control. The heritage of that presence is still strong, in lands such as Bosnia and Spain. Although the Christian West resisted with the Crusades from about 1100 until 1250, the Muslim Ottoman Empire, centered in Turkey, was the dominant economic, cultural and scientific power in the Eastern Mediterranean and the Middle East for centuries, beginning about 1300. It is of interest that Muslims always treated "people of the book," meaning Jews and Christians, better than Christians treated Muslims and Jews. In the Ottoman Empire, the administration nurtured and trained Christians and Jews to be major governmental employees. Jews were given a safe haven from the inquisition in Spain.

The Crusades

Pope Urban II had ambitions to reunite his Roman Catholic Church with the Eastern Orthodox Church, based in Turkey. When the leader of the Eastern Church, Emperor Alexius I of Constantinople, requested help to fight the Muslims who had occupied the Holy Land of Palestine, Urban eagerly seized the opportunity. He aroused the faithful by a dramatic appeal to free the Holy Sepulcher, in Jerusalem, from the Muslims. Thus began the **First Crusade** in 1095, one of several Crusades over a span of 250 years, which were fed by a fanatic zeal to destroy the "infidels."

The Pope's appeal had astonishing success. Several armies from different parts of France were assembled, including the

Provencals led by Raymond IV, count of Toulouse, and armies from Normandy, Flanders, Lower Lorraine, the Norman duchy of Apulia, and Southern Italy. They traveled through Northern Europe, killing and looting on their way to Constantinople, and quickly conquered Anatolia in 1097. Alexius chose to remain there with his army to consolidate his control over this territory, while the Franks advanced to Antioch. After a prolonged siege, Antioch was captured, and the victors, being very displeased with Alexius for not contributing to the city's capture, decided to retain control of it, thus forming a Frankish state in the Near East, and alienating the efforts of the Pope to reunite the Eastern and Western Church. After some squabbling, Bohemund of Apulia assumed control of Antioch. In 1099, the crusading armies captured Jerusalem from the defending Shiite Fatimid forces, who, in turn, had just captured it from the Sunni Turks. Even then, the strife between the different Muslim faiths was detrimental to the Muslim cause. A horrible massacre of both Muslims and Jews in Jerusalem ensued.

In addition to the city of Jerusalem, three other Christian states were established: the countship of Edessa, the principality of Antioch, and the countship of Tripoli. The feudal nature of the government was enhanced by formation of three great military orders of knighthood, including the famous Templars. These knights controlled many of the castles that guarded the frontiers of these states. The caliphs of Baghdad and the sultans of the Seljuk Turkish domains were not overly interested in seizing control of the new Christian states, which encompassed much of what are now Israel, Palestine, Lebanon and Syria (excluding the emirate of Damascus).

These Frankish Christian states were relatively stable for several years. However, when Zangi, the leader of Mosul (in what is now Northern Iraq), captured Edessa in 1144, his threat of a "jihad," or holy war against the Christians, prompted Pope Eugenius III to declare a **Second Crusade** against the Muslims. In 1147, King Louis VII of France and King Conrad II of Germany led armies through Hungary toward Asia Minor, but suffered disastrous defeats at the hands of the Turks. Nevertheless, they did succeed in arriving with small forces in Jerusalem in 1148.

There they made the unfortunate decision to attack Damascus, which was acting as a buffer state between the Turks and Jerusalem. The attack, a complete failure, was aborted after only four days. The far-reaching implication of this unsuccessful Crusade was that the state of Damascus began to question its cooperation with the Franks, and instead favored jihad against the Christians, in alliance with Nureddin, the son of Zangi.

Nurreddin had great military success, first defeating and killing Raymond of Antioch in 1149, then gradually gaining control of Damascus and Egypt, thereby surrounding Jerusalem. Although Nureddin was a Sunni Muslim, and the caliph of Egypt was a Shiite, when Nureddin's Kurdish general, Asad-al-Din Shirquh, rescued Cairo from an invading army from Jerusalem in 1169, the caliph appointed Shirquh as his vizier (advisor). Shirquh died soon after, and was replaced by his brilliant nephew, Saladin, who was destined to become the greatest of Muslim leaders.

Saladin took control of Egypt, and quickly unified the Muslims after incorporating Mosul into his domains. However, his goal of driving the Christians from the area was difficult because the states of Antioch, Tripoli and Jerusalem possessed strong economies and armies, and a superior tactical position along the coast. Saladin cleverly gained some support from the Italians via trade treaties with Egypt, and divided the opposition by utilizing the mistrust between the Byzantines and the Frankish Christians. Meanwhile, the Franks themselves were divided by internal struggles for power. The Frankish army, exhausted by a forced march across the desert, was routed by the Muslims in July of 1187. This defeat left the area almost defenseless, and Saladin took Jerusalem the same year. The Jews and Orthodox Christians were treated well by Saladin and accepted Muslim rule. The wealthier Franks bought their freedom.

Pope Gregory VIII and his successor Clement III succeeded in persuading Richard I of England (the "Lionhearted"), Philip II Augustus of France, and Frederick I of Germany (the Holy Roman Emperor) to initiate the **Third Crusade**, to recapture Jerusalem. Frederick unfortunately drowned in 1190 on his way to the Holy Land. His forces, which were subsequently fragmented, did not play an important role in the Crusade. Philip and Richard, who were at odds concerning English control of several provinces of France, set out together. After Richard conquered Cyprus (because of a disagreement with the ruler, Isaac Comnenus), he and Philip, with the aid of the former ruler of Jerusalem, King Guy, captured Acre on the coast in 1191, and later took several other coastal cities. Thus, the Crusade was a partial success, as it permitted the continuation of part of the former state of Jerusalem. In addition, permission was granted by the Muslims for pilgrimages to the Holy Sepulcher in Jerusalem.

The **Fourth Crusade** was probably the most disastrous of all, as it effectively destroyed the Byzantine Empire, ruining any chances that the Western and Eastern Catholic churches could be reunited. It started in 1199, when several French nobles, led by Count Thibault III of Champagne, set out for the Holy Land via Venice. This is where the problems began, as they did not have enough money to pay the Venetians for the agreed-upon passage via ship. To delay payment of their debt, the crusaders agreed to help Venice capture Zara, a Christian town on the coast of Dalmatia, over the objections of Pope Innocent III. In 1203, after capturing Zara, they further agreed to help put Alexius, son of the deposed Emperor Isaac II Angelus, on the throne of Byzantium. However, the citizens of Constantinople rebelled and deposed the new Emperor and his co-Emperor father in 1204. This led to the disastrous capture and pillaging of the city by the crusaders on April 12, 1204. Although the Byzantines eventually recaptured the city in 1261, their power was at an end. Furthermore, the treachery of the Western Church so inflamed the Byzantines that when finally the Ottoman Turks were on the threshold of capturing the city in 1453, the Greek Orthodox defenders gave up the city to the Ottomans rather than accept aid from the pope.

The **Children's Crusade** of 1212 was an outstanding example of the folly of religious fanaticism. This expedition was not a real crusade, since there was no hope of the young participants even reaching Jerusalem, let alone engaging in any warfare there. Thousands of children and young adults from northern France and western Germany congregated and started marching toward the Holy Land, apparently exhorted to this action by a peasant boy, Stephen, from France, and a boy called Nicholas from Cologne, Germany.

Some of the details of this catastrophe were summarized in *The Crusades: A Documentary History*, by James Brundage, from his translation of the *Chronica Regiae Coloniensis Continuatio Prima*: "Many thousands of boys, ranging in age from six years to full maturity, left the plows or carts which they were driving, the flocks which they were pasturing, and anything else which they were doing. This they did despite the wishes of their parents, relatives, and friends who sought to make them draw back. Suddenly one ran after another to take the cross. Thus, by groups of twenty, or fifty, or a hundred, they put up banners and began to journey to Jerusalem . . . The present groups, moreover, were still of tender years and were neither strong enough nor powerful enough to do anything. Everyone, therefore, accounted them foolish and imprudent for trying to do this. They briefly replied that they were equal to the Divine will in this matter and that, whatever God might wish to do with them, they would accept it willingly and with humble spirit. They thus made some little progress on their journey. Some were turned back at Metz, others at Piacenza, and others even at Rome. Still others got to Marseilles, but whether they crossed to the Holy Land or what their end was is uncertain. One thing is sure: that of the many thousands who rose up, only very few returned."

The Crusades are a perfect example of the exploitation of religious zealots by their leaders in order to achieve goals of personal and ecclesiastical power. These ill-advised wars of the Pope against Muslim states had far-reaching implications, extending even to the present. The statement by the American leadership in 2001 concerning a "crusade" against the Islamic states of Afghanistan and Iraq was especially inflammatory.

5.4 Intellectual and Cultural Power

In addition to controlling the spiritual and moral values of their converts, religious leaders wish to control the intellectual and cultural lives of their followers. Religious dogma dictates many cultural aspects of people's lives, such as sexuality, birth control, marriage, women's rights, and so on. Even in the modern secular state, religious views have great importance. Dogma regarding evolution, stem-cell research, same-sex marriage, and a myriad of other topics is very influential. These topics are discussed in chapters 6, 7, and 8.

Intellectual and cultural power was achieved historically not only in the churches, but also in the religious schools, which were the backbone of human education for millennia. These schools had the potential to create a wondrous and benevolent society. In fact, one of the world's greatest periods of enlightenment, culture, science and religious tolerance occurred from the fourteenth to eighteenth centuries in the Muslim Ottoman Empire, centered in Turkey and present day Iraq. During that period, the Muslim religious schools, the madrassas, were centers of true liberal learning, because they included not only the more traditional religious teachings, but also a wide-ranging curriculum of the arts and sciences. This may have been due to the influence of the spiritual branch of Islam, Sufism, which formed an important part of the teaching philosophy. The combination of two schools of thought, the fundamental and the spiritual, was likely the reason for the success of this enlightened period in religious history.

The liberal education of the madrassas in the Middle East vanished in the nineteenth century, as Sufism declined during the resurgence of the fundamentalist Islamic movement. The madrassas were taken over by Muslim fundamentalists, with support of the wealthy Wahhabis of Saudi Arabia. These fundamentalists, who often preached religious fanaticism, exerted considerable influence on Islamic religious education, not only in Saudi Arabia, but also in the backward and potentially very dangerous breeding grounds for terrorists, Afghanistan and Pakistan (See Chapter 3). This situation led to the formation of the terrorist Al Qaeda movement in Afghanistan from 1980-2000, under the infamous Osama bin Laden, which has proven to be disastrous for moderate Muslim factions, and for relations between the Muslim and Christian nations.

In most parts of the world today, religious schools form only a small part of the education system. However, in isolated cases, such as the madrassas of Pakistan, Afghanistan, and Saudi Arabia, and (recently) the aboriginal residential schools of North America and Australia, their influence has been significant.

Residential Schools

In some countries, notably Canada, it was government policy to "assimilate" aboriginal peoples, in other words, to destroy their native culture and language, in part by forcing their children to attend government-funded residential schools. (See "Canadian residential school system", Wikipedia.org.) These boarding schools were operated by the Roman Catholic, Anglican, Presbyterian, and Methodist churches. The schools were supposed to prepare natives for life in white society. In 1928, a government official predicted that with this program Canada would end its "Indian problem" within two generations. But, the goal of assimilation actually meant cruel separation from parents, and physical, sexual, and emotional abuse for the children. The church-government partnership for aboriginal education lasted from the 1840s to 1969, when the government took over the operation of the schools. The last residential school, Christie Roman Catholic school in Tofino, B.C., didn't close until 1983. It is estimated that one hundred thousand to one hundred fifty thousand aboriginal children attended residential schools.

The first residential school was set up in the 1840s in Alderville, Ontario. By 1920, it became mandatory for all Indian children to attend such schools. The number of schools in operation peaked at eighty-eight. The education was supposed to consist of "training of the mind," and "weaning from the habits and feelings of their ancestors and the acquirement of the language, arts, and customs of civilized life," according to a federal government report published in 1847. To accomplish these goals, discipline was severe in many schools. "Historians suggest that discipline was more harsh at residential schools than at other schools and would not have been accepted in Euro-Canadian institutions at the time. These methods included isolation cells, flogging and whipping, and humiliation"

(Residential School Update, March 1998). Not all residential schools were badly run. Some administrators encouraged staff to learn native languages, allowed visits from parents, and requested more money for food and better shelter for the children.

The Canadian Royal Commission on Aboriginal Peoples started its investigations of abuse in the residential schools in 1991 (final report issued in 1996). Church leaders defended the schools by saying they had the best of intentions, and some natives agreed. For example, in 1975, Dr. Enos Montour, a former residential school student, had noted, "The church meant well. They fed and they educated us . . . it cost them a lot to use their mission money to build those institutions and they kept us alive. I was hungry for four years when I was in there but at least the meals were steady." In 1998, the Canadian government apologized to the aboriginal peoples in a Statement of Reconciliation: "Particularly to those individuals who experienced the tragedy of sexual and physical abuse at residential schools, and who have carried this burden believing that in some way they must be responsible, we wish to emphasize that what you experienced was not your fault and should never have happened. To those of you who suffered this tragedy at residential schools, we are deeply sorry." This was the first government apology, but the churches had apologized for residential school abuse at different times over a number of years. In 1986, the United Church of Canada was the first of the religious organizations to apologize for its treatment of aboriginal children in residential schools.

In 1997, delegates to a United Church general meeting voted to use the word "repentance" rather than "apology" in wording a statement to the native people who attended its residential schools. They were concerned that an apology would mean accepting responsibility for monetary claims by survivors, which they thought should be paid by the government. The first claim against the federal government and the churches for abuse in residential schools was filed in 1990. By 1996, two hundred claims had been received. In 2003, there were about twelve thousand. In 2001, the Anglican Diocese of Cariboo in

British Columbia declared bankruptcy due to residential school settlements

In December 2002, a "fast track" for compensation claims was established to award claimants money based on a points system. It was supposed to save $1 billion and resolve cases much more quickly. About 10 to 12 per cent of former students of residential schools filed lawsuits claiming abuse and loss of culture. It was estimated, in 2003, that there were about ninety thousand living survivors of residential schools. As of March 2003, an average of one lawsuit per day was being settled. Settlements averaged $100,000. This means a total cost to the Canadian government of about $1 billion.

On May 30, 2005, a Political Agreement signed by Minister McLellan and the First Nations Chief Fontaine stated, "Canada and First Nations are committed to reconciling the residential schools tragedy in a manner that respects the principles of human dignity and promotes transformative change; Canada announced today that Frank Iacobucci will work and consult with the Assembly of First Nations and counsel for the churches, in order to recommend, as soon as feasible, but no later than March 31, 2006, to the Cabinet through the Minister Responsible for Indian Residential Schools Resolution Canada, a settlement package that will address a redress payment for all former students of Indian residential schools, a truth and reconciliation process, and community-based healing."

5.5 Personal Power

Popes During the Renaissance

The Roman Catholic Popes of the Renaissance possessed a lust for personal power that boggles the mind. During that period, most lay Christians felt that the Church had become corrupt beyond all reason. Reform was essential, yet the Popes persisted in their ways of greed, nepotism, debauchery and political interference. The powerful Medici family of Florence, who controlled Tuscany for three centuries from about 1450, were generous in sponsoring art and science, but also represented the ultimate limits of corruption in the Catholic church. Their behavior and exploits are legendary in both the advancement of civilization and the corruption of Church hierarchy. The Medici Pope, Leo X, was in power when Luther started the Reformation. According to Barbara Tuchman (*The March of Folly: From Troy to Vietnam*), the Popes of the period 1471-1534 caused this split in the Western Christian Church, which was responsible for so much carnage in the following centuries.

The first in this line of corrupt Popes was **Sixtus IV**, who ruled from 1471 to 1484. He became Pope with the aid of his friend, Cardinal Rodrigo Borgia, who also later became Pope. Sixtus was famous for his nepotism. He appointed 34 of the 39 cardinals, six of whom were his nephews. His nephew Cardinal Riario was infamous for his sumptuous and orgiastic banquets. Sixtus collected vast sums of money, and did some good with it, such as the restoration of the Vatican Library, and construction of the Sistine Chapel. He probably was involved in the Pazzi family's plot to assassinate the Medici brothers.

The next Pope, **Innocent VIII** (1484-92), was a compromise candidate, supported by the future Popes Rodrigo Borgia and Giuliano della Rovere, a nephew of Sixtus IV. Innocent, who was effectively a puppet of Rovere, scandalized the Church by arranging the marriage of his son, Franceschetto, with a daughter of Lorenzo de Medici—of course, Popes were not supposed to have children, as all priests at that time were sworn to celibacy. Their wedding was so sumptuous that he had to mortgage the papal treasures to pay for it. Innocent VIII was the incompetent result of the secularizing of the College of Cardinals. He was the inevitable result of the appointment of cardinals who did not have to be priests, and who sought only personal riches and fame. Many of the cardinals were members of Italy's ruling families. They were known for their carousing, gambling and spendthrift ways. Since Popes were elected from the College of Cardinals, the succession of a corrupt line of Popes was unavoidable.

In 1492, after the death of Innocent VIII, Rodrigo Borgia finally attained his lifetime goal of becoming Pope. He became the infamous **Alexander VI**. He is said to have attained the honor by using unabashed bribery. He ruled for eleven years, in the period following Columbus's famous voyage to America. When elected, he was a man of 61 who had several mistresses and seven children. At the age of 59, he had taken as mistress the nineteen-year-old Giulia Farnese, whose marriage he had just arranged. His reputation was such that the young Cardinal Giovanni de Medici said, "Flee, we are in the hands of a wolf."

Nevertheless, Alexander VI was an intelligent man and perhaps the most competent of the Popes of his era. During his years as a cardinal he helped to arrange the marriage of Ferdinand and Isabella of Spain, thereby uniting the two powerful Spanish kingdoms, and heralding the future glory of a united Spain. The archrival of Alexander was Cardinal Giuliano della Rovere, who tried, with the French King Charles VIII, to oust Alexander for the crime of simony. In 1494, the French army occupied Florence and Naples, and entered Rome. With the help of Spain, which also coveted Naples, Alexander survived the onslaught of the French, and eventually forced them to withdraw. His rule was continuously marred by the attempts of various European powers to control Italy.

In the last years of his reign, Alexander's exploits became more decadent. One famous banquet in the Vatican, called "The Ballet of the Chestnuts," was an amazing pornographic affair, featuring fifty courtesans who danced naked with the guests, picked up chestnuts on the floor while on hands and knees, and then coupled with the guests. Such expensive extravaganzas were financed by the creation and sale of hundreds of new papal offices, including several cardinals.

Reform of the Church was still important for some. One particularly persistent reformer was a Dominican friar, Girolamo Savonarola, who preached that the purification of the sinful clergy would herald a Christian era of unparalleled happiness and prosperity. When he declared that the Pope "is no longer a Christian. He is an infidel, a heretic, and as such has ceased to be Pope," Alexander acted. He ordered Savonarola to be tortured and executed. The Pope did have a brief period of remorse for his sins after his eldest son was murdered, and he initiated some reforms, which were largely superficial.

After Alexander's death, a "good" Pope, Pius III, ruled only for twenty-six days. He was succeeded by the powerful Giuliano della Rovere, who took the title of **Julius II** (1503-1513). He was known as the "warrior Pope." In contrast to his predecessors, he was not so concerned with personal wealth or nepotism. His consuming passions were the restoration, by force, of the Papal States, and endowment of the arts. He organized various military alliances through judicious marriages and political favors to regain lost papal territories. He supported famous artists such as Michelangelo. For such accomplishments, he has retained an important stature in history.

Julius was first allied with King Louis XII of France against Venice, and then became his bitter enemy, partly to thwart the ambitions of the French Cardinal d'Amboise. Julius often personally led his armies, in spite of his aliments. In fact, the austere privations of war seemed to revive his health. In 1510, Julius formed the Holy League alliances with Venice, Spain and Switzerland to drive the French out of Italy. He was temporarily successful, but the tide of war, as always, ebbed and flowed. In the last year of his papacy, when the French armies had conquered most of the Papal States, and were almost ready to occupy Rome, Julius convened the Fifth Lateran Council, in a last attempt to gain God's favor by instituting reform. Miraculously, soon afterwards, his Swiss mercenaries saved the day by decisively defeating the French armies.

Julius' legacies were his destructive addiction to war, and his support of the architectural and artistic revival of Rome. In regard to his territorial ambitions, Erasmus later said, "How do you dare, Bishop who holds the place of the Apostle, school your people in war?" He organized the construction of many new churches and palaces, embellished by sculptures and paintings. Of special importance were his demolition and rebuilding of St Peter's basilica, under the inspired hand of Michelangelo, who also spent four years painting the ceiling of the Sistine chapel. Unfortunately, the cost of these lavish artistic and architectural accomplishments was enormous. To finance them Julius introduced the disastrous "indulgences," whereby sins were forgiven after suitable payment to the Church. In the next papacy, this tithing was to prove fatal for the unity of the Church.

Julius was succeeded by Giovanni de Medici, **Pope Leo X** (1513-21), the hedonist son of Lorenzo the Magnificent. Leo presided over the so-called Golden Age of the Renaissance, an attainment due to his incredibly lavish spending for the arts. Leo's attitude was "God has given us the Papacy—let us enjoy it." Unfortunately, in spite of his education and brilliance, Leo seemed unaware that the corruption and greed of the Church would lead to its collapse during his papacy.

An indication of the degree of Leo's spending was the elaborate wedding he arranged for his brother Giuliano, which cost more than Leo's annual household allowance. Leo also continued the rebuilding of St. Peter's basilica, at enormous expense. He commissioned Michelangelo to reconstruct the Medici Chapel in the Church of San Lorenzo, importing marble from Tuscany for that purpose. But he ran out of money before completing that project. Leo sold more than two thousand papal offices for a sum of three million ducats, which was six times the annual revenue of the Papacy. One of his main sources of funds was the infamous indulgences, which could even forgive sins not yet committed. In this way, the Church actually encouraged sin. There was still a chance for reform in the continuation of the Fifth Lateran Council, which might have avoided the Reformation, but Leo seemed oblivious to the danger.

Leo also indulged in reprehensible conspiracies. One of them was the extortion of money from a group of cardinals, headed by Alfonso Petrucci, who supposedly hatched a plot to assassinate Leo. This whole affair is shrouded in mystery even today. The upshot was that Petrucci was tortured and executed (by a Muslim, as a Christian could not kill a Prince of the Church), and the other cardinals paid large sums of money to avoid prosecution. Leo X also executed other leaders who thwarted his ambitions, such as Gianpaolo Baglioni, the ruler of Perugia, who resisted his domain being incorporated into the Papal States.

Leo was never in good health, and he died a premature death in 1521 at the age of forty-five. His rule was summed up by Machiavelli: "The evil example of the court of Rome has destroyed all piety and religion in Italy." The Reformation was the legacy of his papacy.

After a brief papacy of the reform-minded Cardinal Adrian of Utrecht, which was ineffectual, and only lasted one year, another Medici, Leo's first cousin Giulio, was elected Pope in 1523. As **Clement VII**, he ruled until 1534. During his tenure, The Catholic Church lost Denmark, the northern German states, and much of Sweden to the Protestant movement. When Henry VIII of England requested an annulment of his marriage to Catherine of Aragon, Clement refused because Catherine was the aunt of the powerful Charles V, King of Spain and also the Holy Roman Emperor. And so Clement lost England also.

These were terrible times for Rome and the Church. Clement made the fatal decision to ally with the French King Francis, together with Venice and Florence, to wage war against Charles. The result was that Italy was plundered by a series of armies, culminating in the occupation of Rome by Charles's Spanish and German soldiers in 1527. The Sack of Rome left several thousand dead, countless women raped, and the city in ruin. The Vatican was used as a stable. Clement himself was taken prisoner. Clements' main purpose in his last years as Pope was to restore Florence to the rule of the Medicis. There was much celebration on his death in 1534. His body was later dug up and mutilated.

The Popes of this Renaissance period were largely responsible for the disastrous schism of the Church initiated by the Reformation. They had many chances to reform the Roman Catholic Church, most notably, by the Fifth Lateran Council, but they failed miserably. They not only failed to achieve reform, but it was apparent that they did not even contemplate setting a good example for others to follow. Their lust for personal power and personal wealth outweighed their duty to observe moral Christian principles.

6

———

DOGMA

They must often change, who would be constant in
happiness or wisdom.—Confucius

A man's ethical behavior should be based effectually on
sympathy, education, and social ties; no religious basis
is necessary. Man would indeed be in a poor way if he
had to be restrained by fear of punishment and hope of
reward after death.—Albert Einstein

Religious dogma (tenets, doctrines, canons, "ultimate truths," "natural laws") as well as sacraments and rites, was created by man to provide a basis and a structure for a particular religion. Religious dogma varies widely among the different religions of the world, although some common moral values are ubiquitous. Dogma is not "written in stone" (even the Ten Commandments of the Judeo-Christian faiths exist in different forms within the Bible), but is adaptable. As society and knowledge advance, dogma must change. The rate at which it adapts to new knowledge is a measure of the success and humanity of the religion.

Dogma can be divided into four parts.

1. "Truths" or doctrines that reinforce the particular faith. Examples in Christianity are the first commandment,

———

original sin, the virgin birth, the Resurrection, and the Holy Trinity.

2. Moral codes: The Ten Commandments, The Golden Rule, The Eightfold Path to Nirvana.

3. Behavioral rules, such as the observation of kosher diet and the Sabbath in Judaism; polygamy in Islam; head coverings in Buddhism, Judaism, Islam, and Christianity, and doctrine concerning birth control and abortion.

4. Religious rites and sacraments, such as Communion, circumcision, and various forms of prayer.

6.1 Truths

Religious "truths" are generally myths that have no basis in fact. Examples are the Christian dogmas of the virgin birth, the Holy Trinity, original sin, and (previously) the Earth being the center of the universe. The faithful confuse myth with reality and actual truth. Religious "truths" were created by man, and are therefore subject to human error and prejudice. Dogma is often derived from something written in holy scriptures, which we now know is not the direct word of God, but the creation of humans. These people claimed to have divine inspiration from God, or at least to have obtained that wisdom indirectly. Even if that were true, the divine truths vary from one author to another, perhaps because of errors in translation or memory. For example, the Christian Gospels were not written until decades after Jesus's death, and only a selected few of the many Gospels were chosen to be included in the Bible. Much Christian dogma, like the virgin birth or the Holy Trinity, was created centuries after the time of Jesus, and only after intense internal strife and argument within the Church. Similar arguments apply to the "truths" of other religions.

One of the most famous Christian theologians and evangelists to question Christian "truths" was Charles Templeton—a contemporary and friend of the well-known American evangelist Billy Graham. (See his book, *Farewell to God: My Reasons for Rejecting the Christian Faith*.) He abandoned the Christian faith because of what he considered to be its glaring inconsistencies, untruths, and prejudices, as shown in the Holy Bible. He could not accept the claim that an all-encompassing God would choose a small, obscure tribe of Jews to exclusively bring his message to the people of the world. He could not accept the concept of the Creation, as described in Genesis. He could not accept the concepts of the virgin birth, the original sin, the Resurrection, and the Holy Trinity. He could not accept that Jesus was God. To him, these were ancient myths, suitable perhaps for the insular tribes of the time, but completely ridiculous for modern man. Joseph Campbell, the famous professor specializing in mythology, also debunked many Christian "truths," calling them "evident nonsense" (see Chapter 1.1).

Christian doctrine varies somewhat depending on the group or sect expressing it. The four main groups, Roman Catholic, Eastern Orthodox Catholic, Protestant, and Anglican, all follow the teaching of the Bible, but interpretations of scripture vary greatly. The most conservative Christians believe that the Bible is the actual Word of God, faithfully recorded, and therefore without error. The most liberal Christians believe that (1) the Bible contains many errors, because it was written by human and fallible people; (2) the Bible includes many stories adapted from Pagan religions, like the creation myth and the great flood of Noah; and (3) the authors of the Bible promoted their own beliefs and agendas, which developed over many years. Mainstream Christian faiths believe that the Bible is the Word of God, but also contains passages that advocate unacceptable practices, such as slavery, religious intolerance, genocide, sexism, and racism. They think that, although some of the Bible material is immoral by today's religious and secular criteria, the Bible's creed of justice and love of all people is of central importance.

Such diverse beliefs lead to different concepts of Christian "truths," even including the Holy Trinity—the Father, the Son and the Holy Spirit. This central dogma of Christianity came from the belief that Jesus was the Son of God, and that he gave his life for the redemption of man's sins. In the third and early fourth centuries, there was much discussion about the concept of the Trinity, before it finally became official doctrine in 325. (The

Gnostics rejected this idea completely, as they did not recognize the divinity of Jesus.) Three theologians in Cappadocia, Eastern Turkey, developed the Trinity concept. They were Basil, Bishop of Caesarea; his brother Gregory; Bishop of Nyssa; and Gregory of Nazianzus. They concluded that the Divine Nature or God has a single essence (**ousia**), which is incomprehensible to man, but that three expressions (**hypostases**) of his Being could be known by man, in the forms of the Father, the Son, and the Holy Spirit. These manifestations of God should not be confused with the Divine Nature, or Supreme Being, which is beyond man's comprehension. The Eastern Greek (Orthodox) Church adopted this idea. In the West, the Trinity has always been somewhat less well understood. St. Augustine, who was the most important influence in Western Christianity after St. Paul, tried to define God from a philosophical point of view. He considered that God is a spiritual presence in the human mind, which God has created in his image. As described in his *De Trinitate*, he believed that we could perceive a kind of Trinity in our minds, consisting of memory (knowledge), understanding (self-knowledge), and free will (love). These three parts of the soul "constitute one life, one mind, one essence."

The tenet of the Holy Trinity almost deprived humanity of the wondrous scientific discoveries of Isaac Newton. In his era, the seventeenth century, all professors at Cambridge University had to be Anglican ministers, which meant that they had to believe church dogma. But Newton, who was a biblical scholar as well as a physicist and an alchemist, concluded from his extensive studies that there was no evidence in the Bible for the Trinity. Fortunately for humanity, King Charles II of England was a tolerant person, and turned a blind eye to this religious shortcoming of Newton, and thus permitted him to pursue his research at Cambridge.

A current controversy involving Christian dogma is the myth (truth?), embedded in Genesis, that God created the Earth and all its creatures about six thousand years ago. Also, this myth states that God created man in his image (an egocentric idea). If this myth were true, man did not evolve from apes. For this reason, almost half of all Americans believe that Darwin's theory of evolution is not correct. This theory has been verified by overwhelming scientific evidence from paleontology, geobiology, and embryology, as well as more recent evidence from the genetic sciences. The fact that 98 percent of human DNA is identical to that of chimpanzees is strong evidence that humans and chimps are descended from a common ancestor. It is clear that there are great intellectual dangers in clinging to the idea that ancient scripture is factual rather than allegorical.

6.2 Moral Codes

Moral codes are perhaps the most significant contribution of religion to humanity. However, they are often not obeyed. And, in common with all religious dogma, they are not adjusted over time to conform with new knowledge and concepts of compassion. For example, many Muslims still advocate the death penalty for apostasy. This is a very severe penalty for renouncing one's faith; it is obviously in conflict with a basic human right, freedom of religion.

Of all the moral codes observed by the Judeo-Christian religions (and to a large degree also by Islam), the most prominent are the Ten Commandments, The Old Testament states that the commandments were written on tablets of stone, which were given to Moses by God. Two versions of this event were told. Moses broke the first set of tablets in a fit of rage because the Israelites chose to worship the golden calf. A second set was then given to him. The two versions were handed down to us in Exodus 20 and Exodus 34. They differ dramatically. Either Moses did not get it right, or the chroniclers did not.

First Tables of Stone (Exodus:20) ("which Moses didst break")

1. I am the Lord your God, who brought you out of the land of Egypt, out of the house of bondage. You shall have no other gods before me.
2. You shall not make for yourself a graven image. You shall not bow down to them or serve them.
3. You shall not take the name of the Lord your God in vain.

4. Remember the Sabbath day, to keep it holy.
5. Honor your father and your mother.
6. You shall not kill.
7. You shall not commit adultery.
8. You shall not steal.
9. You shall not bear false witness against your neighbor.
10. You shall not covet.

Second Tables of Stone (Exodus:34) ("the words that were on the first")

1. Thou shalt worship no other god (for the Lord is a jealous god.)
2. Thou shalt make thee no molten gods.
3. The feast of unleavened bread shalt thou keep in the month when the ear is on the corn.
4. All the firstborn are mine
5. Six days shalt thou work, but on the seventh, thou shalt rest.
6. Thou shalt observe the feast of weeks, even of the first fruits of the wheat harvest, and the feast of ingathering at the year's end.
7. Thou shalt not offer the blood of my sacrifice with leavened bread.
8. The fat of my feast shall not remain all night until the morning.
9. The first of the first fruits of thy ground thou shalt bring unto the house of the Lord thy God.
10. Thou shalt not seethe a kid in its mother's milk.

In the second version, there are several commandments that relate to the Jewish kosher diet. The first version is much closer to what is now accepted in the Jewish and Christian faiths. The first four commandments relate to the form of worship for these particular monotheist faiths. The second commandment caused big trouble for Christianity. The Eastern Catholics worshiped images of Mary and various saints, but the Western Catholics claimed that this was forbidden by the Bible. In the eighth century, this dispute inspired the **iconoclasts** (image destroyers) to destroy almost all religious art forms in Constantinople and elsewhere in the East. It was only in 843 that the Empress Theodora restored the veneration of icons in the East. The date is celebrated as the Feast of Orthodoxy in the Greek Church. This dispute was a major cause for the separation of the Eastern Orthodox Church from the Roman Catholic Church in 1054.

The last six commandments are very important and should be obeyed.

(5.) Honor your father and mother. This commandment was also a primary one for Confucianism, which provided a moral base in China for many centuries. In modern Western society, unfortunately there exists a culture of youth, promoted mainly by the advertising executives of large consumer-goods corporations, to promote sales. The respect for elders and parents has consequently declined, to the detriment of our society.

(6.) You shall not kill. This commandment has not been followed historically by any religion, especially Christianity, which has been responsible for countless wars, crusades and massacres. This commandment is interpreted by fanatics as meaning you should not kill members of your own faith, or at least of your own sect. Is it OK to kill Anabaptists or Cathars or Lutherans or Catholics or Muslims? It seems, according to Jesus, that it is not, as he is reputed to have said, "Love thine enemies," "Turn the other cheek." Even today, in the "war" against violent Islamic jihad, many Christians claim that God is on their side, thus implying that it is permissible to kill Muslims. Christians have killed abortion doctors "on the command of God." Some followers of the Jewish faith also flout this commandment, notably in the current Israel-Palestine conflict. The Islamic jihad movement claims that the Koran authorizes killing of infidels. It is sad that this commandment is so universally ignored.

(7.) You shall not commit adultery. This commandment is widely disobeyed today in Western nations, although it is still considered to be grounds for divorce. If indeed marriage is a holy union blessed by God, then there should be some form of punishment, at least spiritually, for adultery. In Muslim states, as is often the case, the religious Sharia law goes to the other extreme, and adultery is still punishable by death, at least for females. (See Chapter 8. Women.)

(8.) You shall not steal. This commandment is largely ignored whenever someone feels he can get away with it. For example, the executives of large corporations in the USA and elsewhere often feel that they are entitled to steal from their shareholders. Perhaps stealing an inevitable result of the Principle of Greed, which seems to be the overriding principle of modern capitalism. Almost everyone will steal small amounts, whether a pencil from their employer or a small amount fiddled in their income tax returns. A return to the observance of this commandment would aid society. Bribery and theft are so bad in many underdeveloped states of the world that Western industries are sought there on account of "Western Trust Capital," in other words, using trust in the West's (relative) honesty.

(9.) You shall not bear false witness against your neighbor. This commandment is basically about lying to further an individual's own interests or to enhance his ego. Who is without this sin? In more serious cases, it can involve lying under oath in criminal trials, and can result in the unjust incarceration or death of the accused.

(10.) You shall not covet. This commandment is closely related to (8.). Among the most infamous violators of this commandment were the Catholic Popes of the Middle Ages, just before the Reformation. (See Chapter 5. Power.) A profound part of the human psyche is self-interest, which is closely related to greed, and it is undoubtedly responsible for many advances in society. In fact, coveting, or being greedy is the basis of the modern capitalist society, which has been so successful in advancing the standard of living, but which could ultimately be humanity's downfall, as the Earth's resources are depleted. Therefore, this commandment should perhaps be modified to read, "You shall not covet excessively." Coveting also refers to excessive desiring of other things, such as a friend's wife, or happiness, or eternal life. Buddhists believe that coveting is the major reason for the misery of man. Coveting is basically excessive egocentric behavior. Reaching out to others, giving love and support to fellow humans, is much more satisfying for many people.

Moral codes of the Eastern religions are basically similar. There are the strict authoritarian codes of Confucianism, which promoted order in Chinese society for centuries; the more naturist concepts of Taoism and Shinto, which encouraged harmony with nature; and the Buddhist Eightfold Path to Enlightenment (Nirvana). The Eightfold Path is a general formula for exemplary conduct; namely, correct belief, thought, speech, behavior, vocation, effort, contemplation and concentration. Correct belief means accepting the four Noble Truths: 1. life is suffering; 2. suffering is caused by craving (**Tanka**); 3. suffering can be overcome by eliminating Tanka; and 4. the Eightfold Path is the way to eliminate Tanka. Correct thought is avoiding lust, malevolence, cruelty and lying. Correct speech means abstaining from lying, blaspheming, vain talk, and talebearing. Right behavior is avoiding stealing, sexual misbehavior, and killing. Right vocation means earning a living without harming any living thing. Right effort is to act on good thoughts and not on evil ones. Right contemplation is being aware of every condition of the mind and body. Right concentration is achieving an elevated state of consciousness by meditation.

Buddhism also observes its own ten commandments, and ten perfections. The Ten Commandments are: Do not destroy life. Do not take what is not given you. Do not commit adultery. Tell no lies. Do not become intoxicated. Eat temperately. Do not watch dancing, etc. Wear no garlands, perfumes, or adornments. Sleep not in luxurious beds. Accept no gold or silver. The Ten Perfections are: Giving, Duty, Renunciation, Insight, Courage, Patience, Truth, Resolution, Loving, and Kindness.

Of all the advice or commandments concerning human behavior that have been provided by religions, perhaps the most succinct, complete, and satisfying one is the Golden Rule, which is a tenet of Judaism, Christianity, Confucianism, and others: "Do unto others, as you would have them do unto you."

6.3 Behavioral Rules

Early religions had very strict rules about almost all aspects of followers' lives. Many of those rules made sense in ancient times, but not today. Around the time when Jesus Christ lived, about 10 percent of all citizens of the Roman Empire practiced Judaism. One reason why Judaism did not become the dominant religion of the known world may have been its excessive rules, which today many consider an infringement on private lives. For example, the kosher dietary rules forbidding the mixing of milk with meat are carried to such an extreme that different cooking utensils have to be used for these different food items. The rules about what a Jew could do on the Sabbath were also very strict—almost nothing could be done on that day, even the cooking of food.

The doctrines of Christian churches opposing **abortion, birth control** and **homosexuality** are not obeyed by many otherwise faithful Christians, and in fact have little or no basis in holy scripture (See *Papal Sin: Structures of Deceit*, Garry Wills, 2000). Early Christian authorities also were ambivalent on these issues. St. Augustine disapproved of abortion, which he called "killing them (fetuses) before they live" (St. Augustine, *On Marriage and Concupiscence*), but only because it thwarted the goal of marriage, namely having children. He was uncertain about when the fetus received a soul, and therefore when it became a person. He suggested that it might have a soul by the forty-sixth day. Thomas Aquinas opposed the baptizing of fetuses, as he thought that they did not yet have souls. In fact, the various churches seem to be confused about abortion. They condemn it on the basis of "natural law," which is of course undefined, but serves to further their goals of control. Abortion is repugnant to many people, whether they are religious or not, because it ends a human life. Whether the life ended was a viable life or not is immaterial. The likely creation of a live baby is ended.

Of course, any method of contraception also ends the possibility of life. Even the rhythm method advocated by the Catholic Church avoids the conception of a life. If abortion were judged to be killing a person, then the Church should decide to baptize aborted fetuses and give them Christian burials. As well, the mother and doctor should be prosecuted. Whether to allow abortion in the case of rape, or to preserve the life of the mother, would have to be decided. The Church is not consistent on these points. Perhaps it should adhere to its area of expertise, and refrain from involvement in judicial and secular decisions.

Regarding birth control, the Roman Catholic Church is clearly out of touch with the populace, even in strong Catholic nations like Italy, since the birth rate there is among the lowest in the world. The precedent for the Roman Catholic position on birth control is contained in the encyclical letter, *Humanae Vitae*, issued by Pope Paul VI in 1968. It stated that the only acceptable form of contraception was the "rhythm method," whereby intercourse was to be restricted to the infertile period of a woman's menstrual cycle. It has been shown medically that this is a very unreliable method of birth control, because, in contrast to other mammals, humans do not signal peak reproductive time (or even realize when it is). In fact, the rhythm method is not only ineffective, but destroys the natural sexual fulfillment in marriage, because spontaneous sexual relations are thwarted.

The Church's position about birth control is based on the ancient idea (borrowed from the Greek Stoics) that all sexual intercourse is sinful unless it is intended directly for procreation. St Augustine stated that "intercourse even with one's legitimate wife is unlawful and wicked where the conception of the offspring is prevented. Onan, the son of Juda, did this and the Lord killed him for it" (*On Christian Marriage*, 55, Encyclical, Pope Pius XI, 1930). Augustine was referring to Onan's use of "coitus interruptus." This biblical passage (Genesis 38:9) does not really relate to birth control, but rather condemns the prevention of producing a male heir, which was then all-important.

Today, some Catholic Churches in various nations permit deviation from the encyclical of Paul VI. The great majority of humans sensibly practice birth control by means other than the rhythm method. Anglicans, at the Lambeth Conference of 1930, decided that contraception was permissible. Judaism, Islam and other religions are not so dogmatic regarding birth control.

Most Christian churches condemn homosexuality. However, this sexual practice is now recognized as a common human deviation, determined by genetic factors. The discrimination against homosexual persons is inhumane, and is contrary to the teachings of Jesus Christ, who reputedly believed in love and tolerance. In socially advanced nations, like Belgium and Canada, homosexual marriage is now legally recognized. However, in nations where conservative, fundamentalist religious views are strong, notably the USA, there is a strong movement against the legalization of homosexual marriage, though it is now authorized in some American states. The objection, where held, has a religious basis, although the biblical evidence for this view is scanty. Homosexuality is not a major issue in either the Jewish Bible (four citations), or the New Testament (three citations from St. Paul[9]). For example, in Corinthians I, 6:9, the crime seems to be pederasty (sodomy), rather than homosexuality. The question of homosexuality is very divisive in some faiths, such as the Methodist and Episcopal Churches. The Methodist Church accepts "gay" parishioners, and even gay pastors, as long as they do not make public their sexual orientation. But if they declare their homosexuality, they are barred from becoming ministers. A major step toward acceptance of homosexuality within Christianity was the founding of the Metropolitan Community Churches, specifically for gays and lesbians. These Churches have grown rapidly. The question of homosexuality is just another example of the reluctance of religious leaders to adapt their dogma to new knowledge and concepts of humanity.

Dogma of Islam derives from its holy scripture, the Koran (Qur'an). In this case, in contrast to the Christian and Judaic Bibles, the word of God was conveyed directly to Muhammad, and was rather quickly written down by scribes (Muhammad

---

9   See *The New Testament and Homosexuality*, by Robin Scroggs, 1983;, and *Papal Sin: Structures of Deceit*, by Garry Wills, 2000.

was illiterate). In addition, much Islamic dogma is based on later interpretations of the Koran and other sayings (hadith) of Muhammad. It follows that this dogma can be modified in time. In Islam, which is much less hierarchal than Christianity, much influence is wielded by senior mullahs, who have proven themselves to be worthy proponents of Islam. These leaders (Ayatollahs in Shiism) make pronouncements that become local doctrine in their spheres of influence.

One of the misinterpretations of the Koran deals with the **hijab**, the covering of women. Hijab means "cover" in Arabic, but Islamic scholars give it the broader meaning of modesty. Muhammad in fact did not say that the faces of women should be covered, but only that males talk to his wives behind a curtain. In one tradition, Muhammad said that when a woman reaches the age of puberty, all parts of her body should be covered except the face and hands. Most Muslim scholars agree with this interpretation. Men are also required to dress modestly, and be covered from the navel to the knees. Rules about women's clothing vary among Muslim nations. In Iran and Saudi Arabia, the religious police punish women who are not covered completely. In Afghanistan and parts of Pakistan, the **burka**, a complete covering, is required. In countries like Egypt, the dress varies widely. Often, younger women have no head coverings at all. In Turkey, it is forbidden to wear the burqa in government buildings or schools. Muslim women in Europe have recently been making a statement of their faith by wearing the **niqab**, or veil, at work or at school. In any case, it is clear that modern fundamentalists in Islam have imposed various oppressive rules on women, including complete female covering. These restrictions make no sense, except to exert male power, and to promote the continuation of ancient tribal and patriarchal customs.

6.4 Religious Rites and Sacraments

Rites and sacraments are important parts of religions. They serve to formalize and celebrate religion. How to pray, and how to observe birth, marriage, and death are rituals that form a structure for society. The religious festivals celebrate religious myths, and cultural events. Christmas celebrates the birth of Jesus, Easter celebrates his death and resurrection, Passover commemorates the deliverance of the Jews from Egypt, Hanukkah celebrates the rededication of the Temple in Jerusalem after the Jewish Maccabees defeated the Greeks, the Muslim Hajj pilgrimage to Mecca affirms the Muslim faith, etc.

The importance of ritual in religion may be misunderstood and underappreciated. Ritual has long been an important part of human existence. It may be a necessary component to ensure mental health. The ritual of not stepping on the cracks of a sidewalk is a well-remembered practice of youth. The ritual training, bowing and salutations in the martial arts such as judo and karate have proven an effective means of instilling discipline and order in young minds. Rituals of bedtime stories, regular mealtime and bedtime hours, and watching certain television programs are family routines representing important parts of the learning experience and the process of growing up. So too, common rituals in adulthood constitute a steadying force. Everyone has a favorite chair to sit in, favorite foods to eat, favorite vacation spots to revisit, favorite games to play, favorite TV programs to watch, and favorite forms of recreation with favorite partners. Such customs or rituals form an amazingly major part of life. They are a stable base on which to lean. Religious rituals may be considered an extension of these everyday habits and traditions.

However, the excessive practice of ritual can culminate in the collapse of a sect or religion. For example, the excessive use of prayer, weird incantations, magic, holy food, secret formulas and severe asceticism probably contributed to the downfall of Gnosticism (see Chapter 2). Eventually such a complicated system of ritual became so oppressive that the religion was replaced by a simpler one, or one that seemed so at the time— Christianity. During the same period in history, Judaism also gave way to Christianity, perhaps because Judaism had just too many rules that good Jews had to obey. Jewish religious law controlled virtually every aspect of life, including the severe rules for kosher foods and observance of the Sabbath.

Christianity also was shattered by its excesses of ritual and sacrament. The Reformation in Christianity, initiated by Luther and Calvin in the early sixteenth century, reflected not only a dissatisfaction with the corruption and moral decay of the hierarchy, but also a need for change in certain Christian dogma, specifically the use of sacraments and indulgences to raise money. The Catholic Church, in particular the Roman Catholic Church, has been particularly slow to modify its doctrine. This is probably due to the enormous power embodied in its hierarchal system of government, which facilitates corruption. The Popes are supposed to have a direct line to God, and be infallible, regarding their official "ex cathedra" pronouncements on faith or morals. There are many examples of ways in which this was not true, and, in fact, many Popes were closer to the Devil than to God. In the period before the Reformation, the Popes of Rome used their power to exact enormous sums of money from their subjects via fees for the sacraments, and through the sale of "indulgences," which forgave mortal sins by suitable payments. The Church was too slow to react to these abuses, resulting in the Reformation, and the disastrous religious conflicts that followed.

An interesting comment regarding religious dogma, as well as the importance of ritual, is given in the book *Islam in America*, by Jane Smith. A recent convert to Islam gave several reasons why he switched religions: "There would be no priests, no separation between nature and things sacred . . . Sex would be natural, not the seat of a curse upon the species. Finally, I'd want a ritual component, a daily routine to sharpen the senses and discipline my mind. Above all, I wanted clarity and freedom. I did not want to trade away reason simply to be saddled with a dogma."

7

SEX

Western Christianity never recovered from this neurotic misogyny leading to women being accused of *"a loathsome and sinful sexuality, which causes them to be ostracized in hatred and fear.*
—Karen Armstrong in A *History of God,*
(in reference to the "original sin.")

7.1 Introduction

In ancient religions, sexuality and fertility were extremely important. Survival of family groups and tribes depended on the fertility of humans. Therefore, some of the most important deities represented fertility. Mother Earth was a deity central to life, as the bounty of animal life and good harvests were essential for survival. Statues of Fertility Goddesses are some of the most common relics of early religions.

During recorded history, religious attitudes toward sex differed wildly. The ancient Druid and Aztec temple priests observed sexual abstinence. Now, celibacy is practiced by Catholic and Buddhist clergy. The early Christian Church considered cohabitation to be sinful (the "original sin"), and only permissible for procreation. Some Christian Churches, such as the Church of the Latter Day Saints (Mormons), originally advocated polygamy, but this policy was revoked as a condition for Utah statehood. Polygamy is still practiced to some extent by Mormons, and fringe Mormon sects, in spite of the reversal of official Mormon policy. Fundamentalist Muslims believe that exposure of any part of the female body will inflame men's passions, so that no part of the female body can be visible in public. (See *Nine Parts of Desire*, by Geraldine Brooks.) On the other hand, in Islam, men are permitted to have four wives, and apparently covet young women or girls, because marriage of women at a very early age is allowed and frequently practiced. The prophet Muhammad was allowed even more wives, by special revelation, after his only and revered first wife died. Judaism has always had a more reasonable, evenhanded approach to sexuality, considering it an important part of marriage. This does not mean that women were given equal rights in Judaism; on the contrary, in common with most of the religions of the world, which have been largely patriarchal, the status of women in Judaism was inferior. In Hinduism, sexual desire is considered to be an essential part of life, and is treated extensively in such texts as the **Kama Sutra**.

7.2 Sexual Attitudes in Christianity

The approach of the Christian faiths has historically been negative toward sexuality, even within marriage. This was not always so, but seems to have been influenced by the Gnostic sects of early Christianity. In the Old Testament, a healthy attitude toward sexual relations was advocated, and in the New Testament, sexuality was not condemned. Jesus had very little to say about sexuality. However, there are a few biblical passages dealing with his attitude regarding adultery, divorce and multiple marriages. In John 8:1-11, Jesus uttered the famous words "Let he who is without sin cast the first stone at her," regarding the imminent stoning of a woman who committed adultery. This story illustrates Jesus's compassion and forgiveness, although he did classify adultery as a sin. There is some doubt about the authenticity of this tale, as it did not appear in earlier versions of the Bible. Concerning divorce, in Matthew 5:31 and Matthew 19:9, Jesus permitted divorce in cases of sexual misconduct. Various versions of the Bible have translated the misconduct as adultery, fornication, unchastity, or marital unfaithfulness. However, according to Mark 10:11-12 and Luke 16:18, Jesus said that divorce is unacceptable for any reason. Regarding multiple marriages, John 4:16-18 records a conversation that Jesus had with a Samaritan woman, "Jesus saith to her, Go, call thy husband, and come hither. The woman answered and said, I have no husband. Jesus said unto her, Thou hast well said, I have no husband: For thou hast had five husbands; and he whom thou now hast is not thy husband: in that saidst thou truly." In this statement, Jesus may have criticized the woman for her multiple marriages, or he may have merely been showing his knowledge of her history.

Early Christians, as well as Jews, believed that the physical world was an expression of the Divine, the direct creation of God, and therefore good. However, with the advent of the Gnostic movement, some old ideas from Persia, concerning the corruption of all material things, reappeared. It was believed that the world was divided into good and evil, and somehow all matter was considered corrupt; only spiritual concepts were good. This philosophy carried over into the powerful Cathar sects of the eleventh to thirteenth centuries in Western Europe. The Gnostics were a very spiritual group, and although they were virtually eliminated by mainstream, Pauline Christianity, some of their ideas persisted. St Augustine was a primary mover in the development of these austere Gnostic beliefs. He considered that only sexual relations that had the immediate goal of procreation were permissible in marriage.

In the myth of Gnosticism, a cosmic catastrophe occurred. The realm of blissful spirit exploded and little fragments of spirit became imbedded in the earth where they became human beings. In the midst of such a catastrophe, how is salvation achieved? Believers are saved through asceticism, by eliminating any attachment to the world of physical reality and by getting rid of emotional involvement and physical pleasure. There is something that is even worse than failing to be detached; namely, bringing more souls or spirits, in the form of humans, into the world of matter. The ultimate evil, then, is to be fruitful and multiply. Carrying this idea to its logical conclusion, one extreme Gnostic sect, the Manichaeans, taught that intercourse with preadolescent girls was not ultimately evil because pregnancy was not possible. Even the Roman Emperors were shocked by this idea and outlawed the sect.

Gradually, the idea developed within this sect that anything to do with conception, copulation or sexuality was evil. St. Augustine was a fringe member of the Manichaean sect for nine years. Even after conversion to Christianity, he retained some Manichaean concepts about sexuality. His book, *The Good of Marriage*, had some extreme views of marriage. Even normal sexual intercourse within marriage could be venial sin, and the sooner married people abstained from all sexual relations the better. For Augustine all sexual acts outside of marriage were mortal sins—acts sufficient to separate people forever from God and so consign them to Hell.

Christian attitudes toward sex have softened in recent years. Now even the Catholic Church believes that sexual relations within marriage are a good thing, and can be practiced without the goal of procreation. However, some natural sexual practices, such as masturbation, are still forbidden. Psychologists believe that masturbation is a normal and natural behavior, especially for children. Since children are sexual beings, exploration of the body is natural. Consequently, nearly all children play with their genitals and many masturbate at the age of two or three. Disciplining children for this behavior is not recommended.

7.3 Celibacy in the Catholic Church

The priests and bishops of the Roman Catholic faith, in contrast to other Christian faiths, are supposed to be celibate[10]. This means that priests should abstain completely from sexual intercourse, since celibate means unmarried, and in Christianity, sex outside of marriage is forbidden. This practice is a regulation, not a dogma, which means that it can be changed at any time on the Pope's command. In the Eastern Orthodox and Oriental Orthodox Catholic churches, married men may be ordained as deacons or priests, but not as bishops, and may not marry after ordination.

The history of celibacy in Catholicism is fascinating. Some of the early Christian disciples, including Peter, who is considered the first Roman Catholic Pope, were married and fathered children. However, the precedent for abstinence was Jesus himself, who was apparently chaste and advocated the sacrifice of married life for the "sake of the Kingdom" (Luke 18:28-30; Matthew 19:27-30; Mark 10:20-21). An important pronouncement was made by the apostle Paul, who recommended celibacy for women in his first letter to the Corinthians: "To the unmarried and the widows I say that it is well for them to remain single as I do. But if they cannot exercise self-control, they should marry. For it is better to marry than to be aflame with passion" (1 Corinthian 7:8-9). In the sixth century, St Augustine, one of the most influential of Christian theologians, became convinced that God had condemned humanity to eternal damnation because of "original sin," and that the guilt of this sin

---

[10] The promise of celibacy is made by the future priest during the ceremony of ordination as a deacon, a stage before priesthood. The bishop says to the candidate "Celibacy is both a sign and a motive of pastoral charity, and a special source of spiritual fruitfulness in the world. By living in this state with total dedication, moved by a sincere love for Christ the Lord, you are consecrated to him in a new and special way. By this consecration you will adhere more easily to Christ with an undivided heart; you will be more freely at the service of God and mankind. By your life and character you will give witness to your brothers and sisters in faith that God must be loved above all else, and that it is He whom you serve in others."

was passed on to everyone through the sexual act. He was not always of this opinion, for earlier he had said, "Lord, give me chastity, but not yet." The concept of celibacy was also powerfully influenced by the ascetic Cathar sect, which considered that all material things, and especially sexual intercourse, were a product of Satan (see Chapter 5.3.1). The Cathars dominated southern France and Northern Italy in the twelfth century, and were wiped out by the Church in the early thirteenth century, but some of their ideas survived.

The official establishment of celibacy for Catholic priests took centuries. From the beginning, Christian priests were encouraged to abstain from sexual contact, even with their wives. At the Council of Elvira in the year 304, it was recommended that all "bishops, presbyters, and deacons and all other clerics" were to "abstain completely from their wives and not to have children." However, at the Council of Nicaea in 325, an attempt to ban priests from marrying failed. Celibacy in the Western Church began to spread in the Middle Ages, perhaps to improve the moral status of the clergy, which was deteriorating because of sexual scandals. A celibate priest would stand apart from the sinful world. In 1018, Pope Benedict VIII responded to the decline in priestly morality by issuing a rule prohibiting the children of priests from inheriting property. A few decades later, Pope Gregory VII issued a decree against clerical marriages. At the Second Lateran Council held in 1139, the first written law that forbade priests to marry was approved. In 1563, shortly after the Reformation, the Council of Trent reaffirmed the law of celibacy. It was not always observed, even by the Popes[11] (see *The Catholic Encyclopedia*, and

---

[11] **Popes who were married**

	Papacy	No. Of Children
St. Peter	32-67	
St. Felix III	483-492	2 children
St. Hormisdas	514-523	1 son
St. Silverius (Antonia)	536-537	
Adrian II	867-872	1 daughter
Clement IV	1265-1268	2 daughters
Felix V	1439-1449	1 son

"Celibacy" in Wikipedia, and "A Brief History of Celibacy in the Catholic Church," FutureChurch.org).

The Roman Catholic Church's position has not changed since the Council of Trent. Celibacy is not an essential element of priesthood (in other words there could be a priesthood which is not celibate,) but it is considered an important part of priesthood, and a sign of the priest's commitment to be free to serve God and his people. In some countries there are exceptions to the celibate tradition. In England, with special permission from Rome, a man may be ordained as a Catholic priest and remain married if he was already married when he converted from the Anglican faith. If his wife dies, he will not be allowed to marry again.

From their beginning, Protestants did not accept celibacy, arguing that it promoted masturbation, homosexuality and illicit

Popes who were the sons of other popes and other clergy:

	Papacy	Son of
St. Damasus I	366-383	St. Lorenzo, priest
St. Innocent I	401-417	Anastasius I
St. Boniface I	418-422	a priest
St. Felix III	483-492	a priest
Anastasius II	496-498	a priest
St. Agapetus I	535-536	Gordiaous, priest
St. Silverius	536-537	St. Homidas, pope
Deusdedit	882-884	a priest
Boniface VI	896-896	Hadrian, bishop
John XI	931-935	Pope Sergius III
John XV	985-996	Leo, priest

Popes who had illegitimate children after 1139

Innocent VIII	1484-1492	several children
Alexander VI	1492-1503	several children
Julius II	1503-1513	3 daughters
Paul III	1534-1549	3 sons, 1 daughter
Pius IV	1559-1565	3 sons
Gregory XIII	1572-1585	1 son

fornication. Martin Luther singled out masturbation as one of the gravest offenses likely to be committed by those who were celibate. He said, "Nature never lets up, we are all driven to the secret sin. To say it crudely but honestly, if it doesn't go into a woman, it goes into your shirt." However, in the seventeenth century, celibacy was adopted by some radical Protestant sects, like the Shakers.

7.4 Sexual Abuse

In recent years, widespread sexual abuse by Christian clergy has come to light. This is just the latest sad tale in the sexual history of Christianity, and is perhaps an inevitable consequence of ancient misconceptions regarding sexuality and its relation to a righteous life. For centuries, the Catholic Church considered cohabitation to be sinful, and only permissible for procreation. The implication was that sexual intercourse was somehow undesirable, or at least that it interfered with complete devotion to God. This strange belief probably originated from the myth of the "original sin" (see Chapter 9). This idea has now been discarded by official Catholic doctrine, which considers that sexual intercourse is a natural and fulfilling part of marriage. However, the decision of the Catholic Church that its priests should remain celibate is perhaps a factor in causing sexual abuse by priests.

A 2004 study by the John Jay College of Criminal Justice, sanctioned by the Catholic Church ("The Nature and Scope of the Problem of Sexual Abuse of Minors by Catholic Priests and Deacons in the United States"), has revealed that in the past fifty years, several thousand children were abused by Catholic priests in the USA. About 4,400 priests have been accused of sexual abuse, representing 4 percent of the 110,000 clergy who served in that period. It is not known how many other cases of abuse were unreported or were suppressed by the Church. These crimes were a horrible violation of the victims' bodies and psyches, and were doubly reprehensible because they also violated the victims' trust in their religious mentors. Moreover, these offences were often hidden by the bishops of the dioceses, who would send the offending priests to a different parish, rather than report the offences to the justice system. By these errors in judgment (which can be considered criminal offenses), the bishops exposed countless more children to abuse by these priests. There are many unanswered questions.

1. Why would priests, who have vowed to uphold Christian laws and principles, stoop so low?
2. Is this abuse more prevalent among priests than the general population?
3. Is this abuse due in part to the requirement of celibacy in the priesthood?
4. Are homosexuals and pedophiles more likely to become priests?
5. Should a "zero tolerance" principle be applied to abuse? That is, should offending priests be defrocked or kept in the church for better monitoring?
6. Should zero tolerance be applied to the bishops who concealed the crimes?

A typical story of unchecked molestation was the case of Father Rudolph Kos, related in the book by Garry Wills, *Papal Sin: Structures of Deceit*, and in the Dallas Morning News, July 25, 1997. Kos had a history of homosexual behavior years before he became a priest. He had abused his own brothers, and an earlier marriage was annulled when his wife told the marriage tribunal priest that "he had a problem with boys." In 1985, shortly after Father Kos was moved to a new parish in Dallas, Texas, his pastor complained to the diocese that Kos kept boys overnight in his room. After the pastor had written to the diocese hierarchy a third time with similar accusations, Father Kos was moved to Ennis, Texas, presumably by Bishop Charles Grahmann, where he became pastor of his own church. Over several years, Kos received Catholic psychiatric counseling, and was classified by a social worker as a "classic pedophile." At last, in 1993, several boys sued Father Kos for abuse. One boy had already committed suicide. The jury awarded the plaintiffs $110 million in damages. Kos was later sent to prison for his crimes.

The financial stability of the Catholic Church in the USA is threatened by the lawsuits emanating from these abuses. For example, in the archdiocese of Los Angeles in 2004, a single abuse verdict awarded eighty-seven plaintiffs $100 million. A huge backlog of five hundred cases still remains in this archdiocese. This catastrophe, of course, erodes confidence in the moral basis of the Church. Catholicism in the USA was already in decline before this crisis. The number of priests and nuns has been in decline for many years. In 1965 in the USA, there were fifty thousand seminarians training to become priests, but that number had decreased to 2,500 by 1999 (from the book, *Papal Sin: Structures of Deceit*).

Similar abuses have occurred in other countries, including Canada, Britain and Australia. Churches other than Catholic also have records of abuse. In Canada, for many years the Church-run residential schools for native children abused their charges physically, emotionally and sexually (Ch. 5.4). Buddhist monks in various Asian nations have also been convicted of sexual abuse.

Sexual abuse by religious groups is not restricted to isolated examples such as these. Certain religious communities, such as fringe Mormon groups and strict sects such as the Amish, have been suspected for some time of systematically abusing and subjugating women. (See also Chapter 4. Cults). In the case of the Amish, who segregate themselves from other communities and practice a strict fundamentalist faith, women are second-class citizens, who must obey all males, including their brothers. They have often been raped by their fathers and brothers, and if they appeal to outside agencies for help, they are ostracized by their families and community. Two such cases of sexual abuse in the Amish community were reported by the television program, Dateline NBC on Dec. 10, 2004.

7.5 Child Brides

According to a 2001 UNICEF report, "Early Marriage: Child Spouses," forced marriages of young girls are a violation of basic human rights. Early marriages subject the girls to a life of isolation, abuse, lack of education, and health problems. In the rural villages of Egypt, Afghanistan, Bangladesh, Ethiopia, Pakistan, India, and the Middle East, many young girls are rarely allowed out of their homes unless it is to work in the fields or to get married. These uneducated girls are often married at ages of seven to eleven. It is very unusual for a girl to reach the age of sixteen and not be married.

Some problems exacerbated by child marriage are poor education, high poverty, a high degree of domestic violence, high incidence of intercourse injuries, high pregnancy death rates, chronic anemia and obesity, and poor health of infants. In developing countries, the leading cause of death for girls between the ages of 15 and 19 is early pregnancy. Education of both parents and children is the most important key to end the practice of forced child-marriages. By providing better education, India has been able to cut child marriage rates by up to two thirds. Girls who are able to complete primary school tend to marry later and have fewer children.

Islam:. The custom of child-marriage existed in Semitic cultures long before the time of Muhammad, but he has been partly responsible for its continuation in the Muslim world today. Muhammad initially had only one wife, his beloved Khadija, but she died a premature death before his historic flight to Medina. Later, at the age of 49, he was encouraged to take another wife, and became betrothed to Aisha, who was then only six years old (see Wikipedia.org). Aisha was the daughter of his closest friend, Abu Bakr. Three years later, when she was nine, following her first menstrual cycle, he married her and sexually consummated his marriage. Before condemning this marriage, one has to realize that in those days, marriage was a political and economic contract, and it was Arab custom to marry very young girls and to consummate the marriage after the girl had her first menstrual cycle, when she was considered to have reached puberty.

Today, puberty (from the Latin, *pubertas*, meaning adult) means the time at which an individual becomes capable of sexual reproduction. In a woman, puberty is often thought to have been reached with her first menstruation (the menarche). However, we now know that the menarche does not mean that the woman is fully developed, and in fact, reproduction can occur only from one to two years afterwards. Therefore, there are no biological grounds to marry such young girls, as they cannot yet conceive children. In fact, the emotional and physical damage done to young brides is sufficient reason to outlaw child marriage. UNICEF recommends setting a minimum age limit of eighteen for marriage.

Muhammad's marriage to a child of nine established an Islamic precedent that a girl is judged to be an adult following her menarche, and is eligible for marriage and sexual relations. Thus Muslim men are allowed to marry and have intercourse with young girls who happen to have an early first menstrual cycle. Clearly, Muhammad erred in this case. This error meant that countless future generations of girls would be subject to this cruel treatment, since good Muslims follow the examples set by Muhammad. There are two conclusions to be drawn from this. The first is that even great prophets are fallible. The second is that religious dogma and customs must change as human knowledge expands.

7.6 Sexuality in Hinduism

Hinduism has a long history of veneration of sexual activity. Hindus traditionally considered that sexual intercourse was the second most important instinct in life, after survival. Elaborate narrations and instructions about how to enjoy sexual intercourse were preserved in verse form in the famous **Kama Sutra**. Almost everyone knows the term Kama Sutra, because humans are all interested, at varying levels, in erotic sex. The Kama Sutra is a **tantra** or chapter of Hindu sacred script written in Sanskrit. Kama, meaning pleasure or desire, was also the name of the Hindu Goddess of Love. A sutra is a precept or maxim or a collection of them.

The Kama Sutra was probably an old oral Hindu tradition before it was compiled in Sanskrit and poetic form by Vatsyayana. The Kama Sutra is considered to be much more than a sex manual. Instead, it is a celebration of sexuality, a spiritual inspiration to aid in the enjoyment of life and the relationship between the two sexes. It is the ultimate sexual treatise of Eastern cultures. The Kama Sutra is an amazingly complete description of kissing techniques, sexual positions, aphrodisiacs, courting practices, and ways of treating marriage (and other) partners. This manual for sexual pleasure has fascinated western cultures for centuries. It was translated into English by the famous Sir Richard Burton in 1883.

7.7 Conclusions

It appears that the Western monotheist religions, Christianity and Islam, have severe problems with the concept and practice of sexuality. In contrast, the Eastern religions, in particular Hinduism and Shinto, have adopted a more sensible attitude. However, some Hindu patriarchal customs, such as the treatment of widows, and the burning of brides when their dowries are considered unsuitable, are barbaric (see Chapter 8.5). The customs of some primitive religions, perpetuated in parts of Africa, also reflect ancient and outdated sexual concepts. For example, the mutilation of female sexual organs is still common in some areas (See Chapter 8.3).

Sexual abuses and retrograde sexual attitudes would likely not be so prevalent if women had more power in religion. The role of women in most religions has been that of second-class members. In Judaism and Islam, women must pray in a different part of the synagogue or mosque. In many Islamic states, women must cover themselves, sometimes completely, leaving no inch of skin or hair exposed, presumably because such exposure would inflame the lust of men. Islam has not moved forward to keep up with the general worldwide emancipation of women, but Christianity has made some progress.

8

WOMEN

Likewise, ye wives, be in subjection to your own husbands.—Peter 3:1

The head of every man is Christ; and the head of the woman is the man; and the head of Christ is God.
—1 Corinthians 11:3

Men have authority over women, for that God has preferred in bounty one of them over another, and for that they have expended of their property. Righteous women are therefore obedient . . . and those you fear may be rebellious, admonish them to their couches, and beat them.
—The Koran, Women, verse 34

Most religions are patriarchal, and therefore traditionally have discriminated against women. Age-old concepts of male supremacy still prevail in many religions. This has had serious adverse effects on the development of human society. Today, suppression of women's rights in some Muslim nations is especially harmful.

8.1 Male-Only Priesthood

The priesthood is denied to women in conservative denominations of various faiths, including Christianity, Buddhism and Islam. Some of the Christian denominations that

---

prohibit female clergy are Roman Catholic, Eastern Orthodox, the Mormon Church, and the Southern Baptist Convention. They all conclude from the Bible that women should be submissive to their husbands, and that they may not assume a position of authority over men, such as a minister or priest. Liberal Jewish groups, including Reform Judaism, have had female rabbis for years. Native American traditional religions have recognized both male and female healers. Most liberal and mainline Christian denominations (e.g., Congregationalists, some Lutherans, the Presbyterian Church-USA, the United Church of Canada, United Church of Christ, United Methodist Church, etc.) ordain women and give them access to other positions of power. Between 1977 and 1997 in the USA, female clergy increased from 157 to 712 in the American Baptist Church, from 94 to 1,394 in the Episcopal Churches, and from 319 to 3,003 in the United Methodist Church.

The Southern Baptist Convention (SBC) is by far the largest Protestant denomination in the USA. They have about 1,600 ordained women filling various roles. In recent years, fundamentalists have won a power struggle with moderates within the denomination. The SBC released a document on May 18, 2000 that stated, "While both men and women are gifted for service in the church, the office of pastor is limited to men as qualified by Scripture." The statement cites 1 Timothy 2:9-14, which says in part, "I do not permit a woman to teach or to have authority over a man." There is no consensus as to the accuracy of this passage. Later in the year 2000, Jimmy Carter, former President of the USA and a Sunday school teacher with the Southern Baptists since the age of eighteen, severed ties with his denomination because of their stance prohibiting women from serving as pastors and requiring women to be submissive to their husbands.

The ban on female priests is Roman Catholic dogma, irreversible by papal decree. Many nuns do not agree with this rule, at least according to the supplication by Sister Theresa Kane, representing the Leadership Conference of Women Religious. When Pope John Paul II visited Washington in 1979, she asked that "half of humankind" be allowed to be "included in the ministries of the Church." The Pope responded that the Virgin Mary should be an example for nuns and she was not a priest. In fact, the papal declaration of 1976 by Pope Paul VI, the "Inter Insigniores," stated that the Church could not ordain women because Christ made only men his original apostles. (However, all twelve apostles were married, but that fact, apparently, does not affect the ruling on priestly celibacy.) That statement is open to doubt, as is revealed in one of the "unknown Gospels," *The Gospel of Mary of Magdala: Jesus and the First Woman Apostle* (Karen King, 2003). This Gospel shows that Mary of Magdala (Mary Magdalene) was one of the original disciples. In addition, in one of the officially accepted Christian Books of the Bible, Romans 16:7, Junia was another female apostle. It appears that Junia and Andronicus were a husband-wife missionary team of the biblical period.

In previous times, the reasons for excluding women from the priesthood were that they were inferior humans, and that they possessed "ritual impurity." Thomas Aquinas set the precedent when he stated, "Since any supremacy of rank cannot be expressed in the female sex, which has the status of an inferior, that sex cannot receive ordination" (Summa Theologiae of Thomas Aquinas, q. 39r). He, in turn, took his cue from Aristotle, a well-known misogynist. Saint John Chrysostom believed that women were just not intelligent enough to be priests. Tertullian (155-220), one of the great early Christian theologians, said that women are "the gateway through which the devil comes" (De Cultu Feminarum, Patrologia Latina 1.1418). The idea of ritual impurity, like many Christian practices, comes from pagan antiquity. Women were considered impure because of their menstruation, which always was a difficult subject for males. In the third century, Patriarch Dionysius of Alexandria said that during menstruation, "pious, devout women would not even think of touching the sacred table or the Body and Blood of the Lord" (Patrologia Graeca 10.12810).

Jesus did not seem to have that prejudice against women, as he mixed freely with all women, including prostitutes and outcasts. According to Augustine, "Lord Jesus Christ arranged that women should be the first to proclaim that He had risen."

—

8.2 Religious Law to Suppress Women's Rights

By ancient tribal custom, women were not given any political
or economic rights. This practice was continued and supported
by organized religious institutions, especially Judaism,
Christianity and Islam, and also by the Eastern religions. In
Christian nations. it has only been in the last hundred years that
women's rights, such as the right to vote, to receive inheritances,
and even to earn a living, have been allowed.

Christianity: The radical change in the status of women in the
Western world during the last century has been lucidly described
by Stephanie Coontz in her book, *Marriage, a History: From
Obedience to Intimacy, or How Love Conquered Marriage.* Wives
used to be treated by their husbands like sexual slaves, servants,
and producers of children. The common practice in Christian
nations used to be that upper-class men divorced wives who did
not produce children, while peasants delayed marriage until the
betrothed became pregnant. It was only after the discovery of
effective means of birth control in the nineteenth century that
women could avoid the burden of bearing numerous children.

Traditional marriage law in both England and America
decreed that. "Husband and wife are one, and that one is the
husband." This law of "coverture" was supposed to reflect
the command of God and the essential nature of humans. It
stipulated that a wife could not enter into legal contracts or
own property. In 1863, a New York court warned that giving
wives independent property rights would "sow the seeds of
perpetual discord." Even after coverture had lost its legal force,
courts, legislators and the public still clung to the belief that
marriage meant entirely different things to husbands and wives.
In 1958, the New York Court of Appeals confirmed the legal
view that wives (unlike husbands) could not sue for loss of the
personal services of their spouses, including housekeeping and
sexual attentions. The judges reasoned that only wives were
expected to provide such personal services anyway. As late as
the 1970s, many American states retained "head and master"
laws, giving the husband final say over where the family lived

and other household decisions. According to the legal definition of marriage, the man was required to support the family, while the woman was obligated to keep house, nurture children, and provide sex. Not until the 1980s did most states criminalize marital rape.

The right to vote was not given to women until quite recently. New Zealand was one of the first Christian nations to permit women to vote, in 1893. In the USA, women had protested for decades, and even went to jail for illegally voting, until finally, in 1920, the 19th Amendment to the Constitution permitted them to vote. However, it was not until much later that black women (and men) could vote in the USA. It is noteworthy that several Muslim nations permitted women to vote and run for office long before Christian nations did. Examples are Kazakhstan (1924), Turkey (1930), Indonesia (1945), Egypt (1956), and Malaysia (1957). Canada did not lift all restrictions on the right to vote until 1950, and on running for office until 1960. Switzerland did not allow women to vote until 1971. ("International Woman Suffrage Timeline," http://womenshistory.about.com)

Islam: (see *Islam in America*, Jane I. Smith.; and *Islam: Religion, History, and Civilization*, Seyyed Hossein Nasr) The rights and legal status of women in the Islamic world, especially in the Middle East, are more restrictive than for women in America, Europe, China or Japan. In the very early stages of Islam, Muhammad supported women's rights. He was very devoted to his wife and he realized that the role of women in his patriarchal society should be improved. Muhammad advocated that all Muslims, including women, be educated. There is however much disagreement in Islam today concerning what subjects are suitable for a woman's education. By such arguments, religious leaders distort the original liberal views of their prophets. Muhammad also made the important decree that women could share an inheritance, an advance in women's rights that far predated this right in the Christian world. However, the present situation in much of Islam is that women inherit only half of what men inherit. Also, in judicial cases, the testimony of one man equals that of two women.

In prayer at the mosque, women must be separated from men, presumably because a close proximity could inflame men's passions. Women are not permitted to be imams, the religious leaders. The main reason is that women are unclean or impure because of their menstruation. Thus, the Christian idea that women are impure and sinful, because of the "original sin," seems to have been carried over into the Muslim faith. Women also do not participate in religious festivals while menstruating. The fact that men may have four wives, but women may have only one husband, also clearly establishes the inferior status of women. Men are permitted to marry Jews or Christians, but women do not have that right. A man may traditionally divorce his wife by simply repeating "I divorce you" three times, but this practice is rarely used today, at least in the Western world. Divorce is less common in Muslim society than in the rest of the world.

According to Sura 4:34 of the Qur'an, "Men have authority over women, because God made the one of them to excel the other [and because men support women financially] . . . So good women are obedient . . . As for those from whom you fear insubordination, admonish them and banish them to beds apart, and beat them." For those who do not treat holy scripture literally, these are indeed harsh words. In practice, many Muslim communities do not consider this Sura to be strictly relevant today.

The role and status of women varies considerably in different Muslim nations, indicating that various interpretations of the laws of the Koran are possible. Often, religious law is cited as the reason for perpetuating the inferior rights of women. In the case of modern fundamentalist Islam, the holy law, or Sharia, is interpreted to mean that women cannot appear in public without a male relative as a chaperone (even in the case of a medical emergency), cannot drive cars, cannot vote, and must cover themselves completely, with only the eyes showing. This is the case in Saudi Arabia, where the fundamentalist Wahhabi sect of the Sunni branch of Islam dominates. The question of women's dress is currently controversial. It seems that the Qur'an did not specify that women must cover their heads, and it has been only recently that head covering (and in some Muslim states, complete body covering) has been required. In Afghanistan under the rule of the fundamentalist Taliban regime, women were not even permitted to attend school or earn a living. Morality police roamed the streets with whips in hand, to punish any transgressions against the strict Sharia laws.

Some advances have been made in recent times. When the Ottoman Empire collapsed in 1919, the inspired leader of Turkey, Ataturk, modernized the nation and decreed that the hijab should be abolished, and that women were to be given equal rights. In most Muslim nations, secular law, rather than the Sharia is observed. Indonesia, the most populous Muslim nation, has relatively equal rights for women. Recently, a woman was elected prime minister. In 2005, Kuwait, one of the most affluent Muslim nations of the world, finally gave women the right to vote and to run for political office. It is always the case in religious matters that the divine words of the holy scriptures are interpreted according to the whims of the political and religious ruling classes of the time—hopefully these classes are becoming more tolerant and wise.

8.3 Mutilation of Sexual Organs as a Cultural or Religious Practice

In several nations of Africa, the sexual mutilation of young females is routinely practiced. This custom consists of severing the clitoris and parts of the labia, and then sewing up the vaginal opening so that only a tiny hole remains. The cutting may be an ancient tribal custom, similar to the circumcision of males in Judaic and Christian cultures. It is likely intended to reduce the sexual desire of the females. The sewing ensures the virginity of the female. (The use of the chastity belt for Christian women in Europe during the Middle Ages served the same purpose.) It is a particularly cruel tradition, as it causes severe heath problems, including infections caused by the inadequate flow of urine. When the female is married, the opening must, of course, be enlarged to permit intercourse. Religious leaders have the power to stop this barbaric mutilation, but have not done so.

8.4 Stoning as Punishment for Adultery

In Judeo-Christian-Muslim tradition, adultery has been punished by stoning to death. This penalty was advocated by Moses, is written in the Jewish and Christian bibles, was practiced by ancient Jews, and is considered by many Muslims to be a part of the Muslim Sharia law. According to the third book of the Old Testament (Leviticus 20:10), "And the man that committeth adultery with another man's wife, even he that committeth adultery with his neighbor's wife, the adulterer and the adulteress shall surely be put to death." A similar invocation appears in Deuteronomy 22:22, with the stoning punishment. However, in common with many ancient, cruel customs, it has been abandoned by the civilized world. One of the first who considered this punishment to be excessive was Jesus Christ, who, in his infinite mercy, said, "Let he who is without sin throw the first stone," when an adulteress was to be stoned to death (John 8:7).

There is some controversy regarding the stoning law in Islam. Sheikh Abdus-Samad Abdul-Kader (Lenasia, South Africa), a member of the Islamic Research Foundation International (see http://www.IRFI.org), contends that there is nothing in the Qur'an about stoning for adultery, and in fact, the easier punishment of one hundred lashes is stipulated there. Allamah Al-Suyuti, the eminent classical Mufassir, has this to say: "The Book (Qur'an) is before everybody and there is no reference to Rajm (stoning) in it whatsoever." After a thorough examination of all the **hadith**s (interpretations of the sayings and will of Muhammad) on the subject of stoning to death, he came to this conclusion: "The assertion that a verse about Rajm was revealed, is based on hadiths that are isolated, and these cannot supersede the Qur'anic injunction (of a hundred lashes) or cast doubt on its purity" (Jalaluddin Al-Suyuti, in *Itqaan Fee Ulum Al-Quran*).

In a recent famous case, the Sharia Court in Muslim-dominated Northern Nigeria sentenced Amina Lawal to death by stoning for adultery. It seems that she gave birth two years after she divorced her husband. The sentence outraged many human rights activists throughout the world, both Muslims and non-Muslims. Amina Lawal would have been the first woman stoned to death since twelve northern Nigerian states began adopting strict Islamic law in 1999. The case aroused so much international condemnation that Nigerian President Olusegun Obasanjo called for her life to be spared, and Brazil offered asylum. (See http://web.amnesty.org, and Wikipedia.com.)

In September 2003, an Islamic appeals court overthrew the verdict. Four of five judges on the court voted to overturn the verdict, citing procedural errors in her original trial. The appeals panel declared her conviction unlawful because she wasn't given enough time to understand the case against her and because only one judge, instead of a panel of three, presided at her trial. Four other women had previously been sentenced to death by stoning in the same region. Three have had their convictions overturned. "We think the death penalty for adultery is contrary to the Nigerian constitution," said Francois Cantier, a lawyer with the French group, Lawyers Without Borders, who was advising the defense. "We think that death by stoning is contrary to international treaties against torture which Nigeria has ratified. We think that death by stoning is degrading human treatment."

It is illuminating to observe that the sentence of death by stoning for adultery, although originally intended for both male and female transgressors, has been applied only to women. This illustrates the continuing subjugation of women under religious laws, reflecting the ongoing patriarchal attitudes of religions.

8.5 The Burning Brides of India, and Widows in Hinduism

The role of women in traditional Hindu society was one of subjugation. For many women in India the situation has not improved in recent years. Most marriages are still arranged by the parents, and brides are often very young. Arranged marriages have been praised in some circles as a more sensible approach than love marriages, partly because of the high divorce rate in Western nations. In fact, arranged marriage in India can be an Eastern version of Hell. First, the bride's parents have to pay a large dowry to her husband's family, in spite of this practice being outlawed by the Indian government in 1961. Then, the bride and her new husband traditionally move in with his parents, who often treat the daughter-in-law as a servant.

Sometimes, the in-laws demand a larger dowry, and if her parents do not comply, she is harassed, and sometimes murdered. A favorite method of killing is the so-called "bride burning," namely soaking the victim in kerosene or cooking oil, and burning her alive. Burning is common because in-laws can then claim it was a cooking accident. The first cases of bride-burning were reported in the late 1900s, but the evil practice has accelerated in recent years, and seven thousand cases of "dowry death" were reported in the year 2005.

Some women have started movements against bride-burning, and have received media attention. One example is Appa Shahjihan, whose daughter Mooni was burned to death in 1986 by her in-laws when her parents refused to give them more dowry money. Appa claims that police laughed when she sought justice for her daughter's death. Her response was to open a shelter and support office for victims of dowry abuse.

In traditional Hinduism, a widow was considered partly responsible for her husband's death. After his death, she had three choices—to be cremated along with her husband, to remain chaste for the rest of her life, or to marry the younger brother of her dead spouse. The custom of **suttee**, the immolation of a widow on her husband's funeral pyre, was outlawed by the British in 1829. Remarriage of widows became legal later in that century. In India today, there are about 34 million widows. Most of these are still bound by the ancient Hindu traditions, which are basically patriarchal. Many impoverished widows live in **ashrams**, which are Hindu residences, like convents, for worship and contemplation. Others remain as unpaid servants in the households of their in-laws, since a woman traditionally becomes the property of her husband's family. Widows were often forced to have sex with men in their husbands' families, or to sell sex. This practice was once so widespread that the Hindi word "randi," or widow, came to mean prostitute. (See the film "Water," directed and written by Deepa Mehta, 2005.).

8.6 Gang Raping as Tribal Punishment in Muslim Societies

In his editorial, "Sentenced to Be Raped" (New York Times, Sept. 29, 2004) Nicholas Kristof dramatically described a common brutal custom of some Muslim tribes. When a clan considers that it has been wronged by a person from a different clan, usually from an economically lower class. the aggrieved clan members "sentence" a sister of that person to be raped by a group of the offended clan's members. This is unusual and cruel punishment, not only because of the rape, but also because the humiliation and shame of this rape means that the raped woman usually commits suicide soon afterward.

A specific example of this punishment occurred recently in Meerwala, Pakistan. The police record states that, in June 2002, members of a high-status tribe sexually abused a brother of Bibi Mukhtaran, and then tried to conceal their crime by falsely accusing him of having an affair with a high-status woman. The village's tribal council decided to punish him through his sister, Bibi, by having her publicly raped by members of the high-status tribe. After that, she was forced to walk home naked in front of three hundred villagers. In Pakistan's conservative Muslim society, Ms. Mukhtaran's shame meant that she was duty bound to commit suicide. However, she bravely brought her rapists to trial, and they were actually convicted, and sentenced to death. This occurred only because the government of General Musharraf, which was trying to restrict the power of fundamentalist Muslims, decided to make an example of this case. Furthermore, president Musharraf gave Ms. Mukhtaran $8,300 and ordered police protection for her.

Ms. Mukhtaran, who had never gone to school herself, made the wonderful decision to use the money to build two schools in her village, one for girls and another for boys, because she believes that education is the best way to achieve social change. She is perfectly correct in that conclusion, and is to be commended for her altruism. The girls' school is named for her, and she is now studying in its fourth-grade class. "Why should I have spent the money on myself?" she asked, adding, "This way the money is helping all the girls, all the children."

Such cases as this, which receive international attention, can have far-reaching results. In August 2005, the Pakistani government awarded Mukhtaran the Fatima Jinnah gold medal for bravery and courage. In November 2006, Pakistan's Parliament voted to move its rape laws from religious law to the secular penal code. It also changed the rape law so that the victim no longer had to produce four witnesses to the assault, and it allowed circumstantial and forensic evidence to be used for investigation. This effectively separated rape from adultery, and therefore freed women to accuse rapists. Previously, it was almost impossible to get a rape conviction because four witnesses were required. If rape was not proven, the woman would be convicted automatically of adultery.

9

SIN

Let he who is without sin throw the first stone.
—Jesus Christ (John 8:7)—the authenticity is
questionable, but the concept is pure Jesus.

9.1 Overview

Religions have a great deal of trouble coping with sin and evil. They have difficulty with the idea that God made an imperfect universe, and that the world is beset with problems. Why do natural catastrophes, such as floods, earthquakes, forest fires, pandemics and famine occur? Why are humans imperfect, and often sinful, if not downright evil? How could God have created chaos and evil?

One approach was that there were two Gods, a good God and an evil God. Sometimes the evil God was considered to be a "fallen angel." This concept was adopted by the powerful Gnostics and Manichaeans, who believed basically that all matter, including man, was evil and corrupt. Only man's soul was pure. Consequently, their ultimate goal was to sever their souls from their bodies and the rest of this material world, so that their souls could ascend to the perfect Heaven. These ideas created a lot of "Angst" in the budding religion of Christianity, as the mainstream Pauline Christians could not tolerate the idea of two Gods, and especially of an evil God. They solved

------

the sin part of the dilemma (but not the imperfect world part) by adopting the idea of "original sin," whereby man was perfect to begin with but was perverted by Satan. A difficulty with this concept is that every newborn baby is born a sinner, and can be redeemed only by baptism. Consequently, those unfortunate souls who are not given the opportunity to be baptized before dying are condemned to the eternal fires of Hell. It is difficult to reconcile this fate with the concept of a loving God.

Other religions, such as Judaism, on which Christianity is based, do not believe that man is basically born evil. The Christian concept of original sin resulted from the temptation of Eve in the Garden of Eden, as written in Genesis, the first book of the Jewish Torah. Judaism, however, teaches that man has a tendency toward sin, but is not forever tainted by original sin. In fact, a Jewish benediction states, "My God, the soul which Thou hast given me is pure" (Talmud, Berachoth 60b). Moreover, Jews believe that the body is also pure: "Nothing in the human body is unclean; all of it is pure."

Buddhists believe that all problems of humanity are caused by the lusts and desires of man. The first two Noble Truths are that life is suffering (including the trauma of birth, the pain of sickness, the loss of loved ones, the decrepitude of old age, and the fear of death), and that the cause of suffering is **Tanka**, which is desire or selfish craving. Tanka is overcome by following the Eightfold Path to **Nirvana** (Enlightenment), consisting of correct belief, resolve, speech, behavior, occupation, effort, contemplation and concentration. Basically, to achieve Nirvana, man must eliminate all desires, including the lust after success and money, carnal desires, and even the desire to eat, drink and breathe air to survive. However, the so-called "Buddhist paradox" arises because all desires are not eliminated if the desire to attain **Nirvana** still remains. Consequently, some **Bodhisattvas** (holy men) decide to return to earth as mere mortals, giving up even the desire for Nirvana. The Buddhist concept of equating sin with desire is not reasonable, since various human desires are the basis for all advances in humanity, including the desire for improving man's quality of life and the desire to ensure a safe environment. Since man's continued existence depends on carnal lust, it would be difficult to argue that it is sinful ("Be fruitful, and multiply," said the sensible Jews).

In earlier times, the behavior of everyone was stipulated rigidly by his religion. Disobedience of any of the many rules and laws of the religion was considered a sin, punishable in this life to various degrees. More importantly, a sin could lead, in the afterlife, to the everlasting fires of Hell. Today, it is a religious sin to disobey a religious moral dictum or commandment. (It is not necessarily a secular sin, as with adultery). In general, religious "commandments," such as the ten commandments of Christianity, contribute to social order and lawful societies. However, since religious laws and codes are formulated by man, they are subject to error. Even when they are supposed to be given to man directly by the word of God, man has to write them down, and later they are interpreted in different ways by religious scholars. For example, the many laws of Judaism were originally provided by God in the Torah, but then were developed over a period of many centuries by religious scholars to form the Talmud, the practical moral code and rules of conduct for Jews. The same process applies for all religions.

In many religions, it is considered a serious sin to question the dogma of the church. Apostasy, or renunciation of a person's faith, is the most serious such offence. In Islam, it is punishable by death. It is also a sin to blaspheme a religious prophet. As a recent example of this, Ayatollah Khomeini, the recent spiritual leader of Iran, condemned the author, Salman Rushdie, to death for his reference to the "Satanic Verses" of Muhammad, in Rushdie's book of the same name. The verses in question are a disputed part of Muhammad's preaching, in which he presumably suggested that the worship of some of the old gods of the Arabs, instead of exclusive worship of Allah, would be permissible. It seems that even to mention this possibility is a severe transgression.

Historically, deviation from the accepted set of religious dogmas in the Christian Church was also punishable by death, and, in fact, often the gruesome death of being burned alive. Jean d'Arc, the famous French patriot, who led the French armies against the English in the Middle Ages, was a prime example of such a brutal and non-Christian act. Many devout Christians, who adopted slightly different ideas of what Christianity should entail, suffered the same fate. The Anabaptists, who believed that infants should not be baptized, were perhaps the most persecuted sect in history. Jews were vilified for centuries by Christians because of the mistaken dogma that all Jews through eternity were to be punished for their supposed part in the crucifixion of Jesus.

Today, in most religions, God will forgive sins, especially if the sinner is truly repentant. Most Christians believe that both repentance and forgiveness of others are necessary for God's forgiveness. For example, from Matthew 6:14,15: "If you forgive those who sin against you, your heavenly Father will forgive you. But if you refuse to forgive others, your Father will not forgive your sins." In the Catholic Church the power to forgive sins is vested in the Church authorities. A Catholic can atone for his sins by the sacrament of penance, which includes confession of his sins to a priest, asking for forgiveness and undergoing certain penalties. For most Protestants, only God and Christ can forgive sins. Jews believe that doing good works will compensate for sinful behavior. Allah accepts the sincere repentance of those who turn to him for forgiveness: "whosoever forgives and makes amends, his reward is upon Allah"(Qur'an 42:40). In Hinduism forgiveness is considered the highest virtue.

9.2 Original Sin

The Christian concept of the Original Sin came from Genesis, the first book of the Jewish and Christian bibles. It seems that Eve, tempted by Satan, ate the forbidden fruit, and persuaded Adam to do the same. That was the start of all man's problems. This act of consuming the Apple from the Tree of Wisdom is supposed to have introduced both sin and mortality to the human race. The guilt was passed on to every man through the sexual act. According to St. Augustine, this transgression caused God to condemn humanity to eternal damnation. Scholars believe he based this idea on the passage, Romans 5:12: "Wherefore, as by one man sin entered into the world, and death by sin; and so death passed upon all men, for that all have sinned." This hardly seems fair. The transfer of responsibility for a sin to all future generations is not accepted today. The idea of the Original Sin is one of the major tenets of Christianity, for Jesus sacrificed himself to redeem all men from this Sin. It is believed by some that without the Original Sin, Jesus's sacrifice would have no meaning, and the whole basis of Christianity would vanish.

Eastern Orthodox Christians, Jews and Muslims did not adopt this concept of the Original Sin. Modern liberal Christians also do not believe this literal interpretation of Genesis 3. They believe that the Garden of Eden story is an allegory, illustrating the maturing of each individual. They even suggest that the eating of the forbidden fruit was beneficial, as it taught man (and woman) a moral sense. Thereby Adam and Eve advanced from an animal state to becoming full-fledged human beings. This was the viewpoint of the Gnostic sect of Christians, who were vanquished by the Pauline sect that formed the basis of modern Christianity

Women in early Christianity were not blamed for the original sin; only later, under the influence of St. Augustine and others, were women considered evil. Tertullian's view of women was "You are the devil's gateway . . . You so carelessly destroyed man, God's image. On account of your desert, even the Son of God had to die." Karen Armstrong in her brilliant book, *A History of God*, expresses this opinion: "Western Christianity never recovered from this neurotic misogyny" leading to women being accused of "a loathsome and sinful sexuality, which causes them to be ostracized in hatred and fear. This is doubly ironic, since the idea that God had become flesh and shared our humanity should have encouraged Christians to value the body."

9.3 Punishment for Sins

Islam:

The Islamic scholar Ibn Masud states, "The blood of a Muslim person is not permissible except in one of three situations: the adulterer who is married, one who has killed unjustly, and the apostate." The Sharia law specifies the following penalties for specific "violations against sacred things:"

1) **Taking Human life**—the penalty is execution, if the heirs of the murdered person do not forgive the murderer, nor accept compensation.
2) **Purity of Lineage**—the penalty is stoning to death or one hundred lashes for fornication, adultery or abortion.
3) **Apostasy**—the penalty is death.
4) **Human intellect**—the penalty is one hundred lashes for consuming intoxicants and alcoholic beverages since they affect the mental faculty, create dependency, harm the body and pose immense danger to society.
5) **Respect and honor of citizens**—the penalty is eighty lashes for slander and false accusations regarding a person's chastity.
6) **Property**—the penalty is amputation of hand or foot for theft or looting.

Evidence required to prove adultery is either an uncoerced confession or the testimony of four **males** who witnessed the act "as the pen enters the inkpot."(If video footage is provided, a lighter sentence will be imposed, not stoning.) Consequently, when a woman is raped, she does not dare to press charges, as she will be punished for adultery if she cannot produce the four male witnesses. In parts of the Muslim world, these severe Sharia laws are not practiced.

Christianity:
Traditionally, the fires of Hell were considered the ultimate punishment for severe sins. Excommunication was also a feared penalty in earlier days, and still occurs today. As with Islam, the Bible specifies stoning to death for adultery. Many of the secular laws of Christian nations are based on scripture. Punishments vary in different nations. The death penalty is still the punishment for murder in some nations, like the USA.

Hinduism:

The Hindus have a different way of punishing a sinner. He will be reborn in his next life as an inferior life form. Hindus believe in the Law of Action, called **Karma**, which dictates that "From good must come good, and from evil, evil." As a result of good deeds, a believer is reborn in a higher caste, and as a result of bad deeds he is reborn as an inferior being, perhaps in a lower caste or as a lower life form—an animal or insect. The caste system placed the Brahmans or priests on top, followed by soldiers, then artisans, then peasants, and finally the "untouchables."

9.4 Summary

Religions have a different concept of sin than does the general public. The basic moral codes that religions preach are accepted by most people. But many religions cling to some out-of-date ideas of what constitutes sin. Some examples are: (1) adultery and homosexuality are condemned by both Christian and Muslim churches; (2). Islam considers apostasy an extremely serious sin, punishable by death; (3) such an innocent thing as improper dress is a sin according to some fundamentalists, especially in Islam. These examples illustrate the main problems that beset religion: (1) rigid adherence to old dogma, (2) the lust for doctrinal power, and (3) the plague of fanaticism.

10

BENEVOLENCE

Love your neighbor as yourself
—Old Testament—Leviticus 19:17

Virtue is to love men. And wisdom is to understand men.
—Confucius

Do unto others as you would have them do unto you.
—Golden Rule of Christianity

Kindness is the golden chain by which society is bound together.
—Goethe

Most religions are based on lofty ideals. The hope for religion is that benevolent attitudes will prevail over the chief evils of religion, namely the lust for wealth and power, rigid dogma, and fanaticism. Religion has enormous potential to benefit mankind. Much good has been done through religious organizations, such as the Salvation Army, the Catholic Charities Network, boys' camps, hospitals, and schools. An important organization, The World Council of Churches, which includes 293 member denominations representing four hundred million people, is the strongest religious organization supporting world peace and the ecumenical movement.

Religions were not always benevolent. Many of the ancient religions, permeated by fear of the unknown, invented powerful, vengeful Gods that controlled many of the forces of nature, such as thunder, storm, the sun and demonic animals like dragons. In an extension of this idea, the early monotheist Gods of Judaism and Zoroastrianism were a severe lot, promising the everlasting fires of Hell for transgressions, but also rewarding the good with visions of Heaven, or, in the case of Hinduism, reincarnation as a higher-level mortal. Early religions also practiced sacrifices of animals and humans to appease the Gods.

The Jewish God, Yahweh, punished the Egyptians fearsomely, with plagues, killing of firstborn males, etc., presumably for not letting the Jews leave Egypt. When Yahweh considered that his people were not pious enough, or had sinned in various ways, he wiped them all out in the great flood that Noah survived. On the other hand, Judaism today praises good works and love above all. Most religions today try to do good, and help those in need.

10.1 Christian Charities and Organizations

Important aspects of religions are the sense of community and aiding the less fortunate members of that community. Both within and outside their congregations, many religions contribute an enormous amount of good works through charitable organizations. When international disasters, such as earthquakes, floods or famines occur, religious organizations are the first to offer help. Churches have been accused of proselytizing after these disasters, in conflict with the International Red Cross guidelines. However, because of religious enthusiasm, it is often difficult to avoid the mixing of charity with attempts at conversion.

Pax Christi International is a Catholic movement, organized originally in Europe in 1945, to promote reconciliation at the end of the Second World War. It is now an international organization, concerned with human rights, peace, justice and ecology. It consists of autonomous national sections, local groups and affiliated organizations spread over more than thirty countries and five continents with more than sixty thousand members. The Secretariat's office is in Brussels. It has representation status at the United Nations in New York and Vienna, the UN Human Rights Commission in Geneva, UNESCO in Paris, UNICEF in New York, and the Council of Europe in Strasbourg. The goals of Pax Christi International are reconciliation in conflict areas, promoting human rights, justice and disarmament, and networking with other peace-seeking organizations.

The Salvation Army, an evangelical Christian charity, was founded in 1865 by William Booth in London, England. In 1878, the leaders cleverly adopted a quasi-military command structure, and named their organization The Salvation Army. This apparently aided the rapid development of the charity. Today the Army retains certain soldierly features such as uniforms, flags and ranks to identify its members. Officers of the Army, led by the General, are recognized ministers of religion. "All Salvationists accept a disciplined and compassionate life of high moral standards which includes abstinence from alcohol and tobacco. From its earliest days, the Army gave women equal opportunities, every rank and service being open to them. All members are encouraged to love and serve God." It operates in more than one hundred countries. Its avowed goals are "the advancement of the Christian religion . . . of education, the relief of poverty, and other charitable objects beneficial to society or the community of mankind as a whole. Its message is based on the Bible. Its ministry is motivated by the love of God. Its mission is to preach the gospel of Jesus Christ and to meet human needs in His name without discrimination."

According to the Salvation Army's Web site, as of 2002, their activities worldwide had 107,724 employees, one million senior soldiers, 398,500 junior soldiers, twenty-nine thousand senior band musicians, seventy-one thousand senior songsters, 546,414 beneficiaries, and 1,400 thrift shops. The social programs included residential accommodations for eighty thousand homeless, elderly, street children, and emergency cases. Day care facilities supported forty thousand for early childhood education, street children, and elderly. Centers for drug addiction served forty thousand.

The Catholic Charities Network of the USA has a long history, beginning in 1727 when the French Ursuline Sisters opened an orphanage in New Orleans. The Network is ranked as the third largest nonprofit charity in the USA. In their 2003 annual survey, the Network reported that they offered food services to 4.5 million people, family assistance and counseling services to 1.2 million people, community services, including health, education and social support to 3.1 million people, and housing services to five hundred thousand people. The budget was almost three billion dollars, of which 60 percent was provided by the government. This is a very large organization, employing fifty thousand paid staff and 200,000 volunteers.

The World Council of Churches (WCC) is the principal international Christian ecumenical organization. Based in Geneva, Switzerland, it has a membership of 342 churches. After the initial successes of the Ecumenical Movement in the late nineteenth and early twentieth centuries, including the Edinburgh Missionary Conference of 1910, church leaders in 1937 agreed to establish a World Council of Churches. Its official establishment was deferred with the outbreak of World War II until 1948. Representatives of 147 churches assembled in Amsterdam to merge the Faith and Order Movement with the Life and Work Movement. Subsequently, mergers were with the International Missionary Council in 1961 and the World Council of Christian Education (with its roots in the eighteenth century Sunday school movement) in 1971. WCC member churches include nearly all the world's Orthodox churches, numerous Protestant churches—such as Anglican, Baptist, Lutheran, Methodist, and Reformed churches—and a broad representation of united and independent churches. The largest Christian denomination, the Roman Catholic Church, is not a member of the WCC, but has worked closely with the Council for more than three decades and sends observers to all major WCC conferences as well as to its Central Committee meetings and the Assemblies. The Vatican's Pontifical Council for Promoting Christian Unity also nominates twelve members to the WCC's Faith and Order Commission as full members. Representatives of the member churches meet every seven years in an Assembly, which elects a Central Committee that governs between Assemblies. One commission concentrates on the promotion of justice, peace and ecology, especially in relation to young people, women, indigenous peoples and racially and ethnically oppressed people. Focal issues have been globalization and the emergence of new social movements.

10.2 Muslim Charities

Ironically, one of the most effective charitable activities of the Muslim world was the creation of the madrassas, or religious schools, which recently have been associated with terrorism and jihad. In recent years, madrassas have supported and educated the poor in nations like Afghanistan and Pakistan. The education is largely religious, and is in many ways similar to that of parochial Christian schools. Unfortunately, in the last twenty-five years, many madrassas have come under the control of the Wahhabi sect of Saudi Arabia, which is not only somewhat fanatical in its fundamentalist approach to Islam, but also encourages hate of the West and Christianity.

A similar shadow has been cast over Muslim charities in general, as a few of them have concealed financial support for terrorist activities. However, many legitimate Muslim charities exist in the USA and abroad. The organization called **LIFE for Relief and Development** is one of the largest American Muslim charities. It operates legally and in conjunction with many government agencies. LIFE is a nonprofit, nongovernmental organization which cooperates with the Economic and Social Council of the United Nations and is registered with United States Agency for International Development (USAID). LIFE offers a variety of humanitarian, health, educational and emergency programs. Two other prominent Muslim charities are **Islamic Relief** and **Muslim Aid**.

11

HOPE

I do not feel obliged to believe that the same God who has endowed us with sense, reason, and intellect has intended us to forgo their use.—Galileo Galilei

Work out your own salvation. Do not depend on others.
—The Buddha

Is there hope for the future of religion? Religion has had a stormy history, which is to be expected, since it is an invention of man. It has developed from a collection of superstitions, based on myth and fear, into a myriad of sophisticated moral, spiritual and social institutions. Enormous difficulties have hindered the full realization of its potential to benefit mankind. Most of these difficulties are based, of course, on the frailties, insecurities and lusts of man. Chief among these flaws is the lust for power, in many forms, such as personal, sexual, cultural, spiritual, and territorial power, as described in Chapter 5. It has been exacerbated by an overly rigid adherence to outdated dogma (Ch. 6.), and by the fanaticism (Ch. 3.) that seems to be an inevitable result of an unquestioning faith. These human flaws have led to enormous harm, in the form of persecutions, sexual abuse, inquisitions and wars, effectively negating the benevolence and good works of many religious groups. These transgressions do not have to continue. Religious leaders and laity in the modern era can overcome them by embracing liberal education, democratic reform, renewed spirituality, and ecumenical cooperation.

Dogma

Religious dogma has hindered the development of scientific advances through the ages, because it is often obsolete, being based on ancient and patriarchal concepts. How can dogma be made more adaptable, or at least put in a form that will not lead to direct conflict with science? One example of such conflict was the early Christian insistence that Earth was the center of the Universe. This really had nothing to do with spirituality, the concept of God, or any basic religious concept. It was clearly the misguided idea of some religious leaders. The famous Italian astronomer and scientist, Galileo, was convinced by his observations of the movement of planets and stars, together with the earlier observations of Copernicus, that the earth in fact revolved around the sun. Galileo's findings were a shock to the clergy, who stubbornly refused to accept the scientific facts. He was eventually forced to recant his beliefs to avoid the penalty of death. The Roman Catholic Church eventually did accept his findings, but only centuries later. This process could have been accelerated if the minds of the clergy had not been stultified by their early years of rigid religious education, if the clergy had communicated in an open manner with the scientists, and if a council of religious leaders, politicians and scientists had been assembled to discuss a reasonable solution,

Actually, religions have sometimes supported science, and when they did, civilization advanced. The Muslim Ottoman Empire of the Middle East, with its relatively liberal madrassa school system, was a good example of the benefit arising from religious support for scientific knowledge. Ancient Chinese regimes, strongly influenced by the naturist Taoism, and having good communication among their three religions—Taoism, Confucianism, and Buddhism—approved of and supported empirical science. In Christian Europe, considerable important research was done at monasteries, notably the great discoveries of Mendel, which were the birth of modern genetic science. Today, the Roman Catholic Church has shown that it is not averse to science. It has even sponsored astronomical research, including an observatory near Rome. Unfortunately, some present Christian sects that claim to be science-oriented, such as Christian Science, Scientology and Science of Mind, have mostly adopted pseudoscience, which is equivalent to myth.

In Europe during the seventeenth and eighteenth centuries (the Ages of Reason and Enlightenment), improved education and more democratic and secular governments contributed to a feeling that science could explain our world better than religion. The result was that faith in religion suffered a serious setback. The effects still remain in Europe, where the popularity of religion has been declining for decades. The struggle of religion against logic and empirical science is still going on, with religious opposition to stem-cell research, gene therapy, and even the concept of the evolutionary development of mankind. Apparently, religious leaders have not learned from earlier mistakes.

In the meantime, both religious and nonreligious people have realized that science cannot explain everything. The origin of the universe is a mystery, and probably will always be. Moreover, humans have been disillusioned by the fear that scientific discoveries can potentially destroy mankind. This may help to explain the present rapid spread of new religions, as well as the resurgence of more conventional religions in China, India, and Africa. In spite of all, religion is alive and well. It seems that the inspiration, community support, and spiritual concepts of religion appeal to humans, especially in regions of the world where people are poor and oppressed.

If the world's religions wish to remain strong and relevant, their doctrines must be adapted to modern concepts. Religious dogma has indeed evolved through the ages, both as a result of new knowledge, and as a result of some changes in human psychology. In early times, society was controlled by instilling in man the fear of the wrath of God, and the threat of eternal damnation in Hell for transgressions. But this approach is no longer effective. Religious myths are less believable today, because of the dissemination of knowledge. Although religious codes of morals and ethics have always been useful to control the base instincts of man, they must be modified now by the knowledge and pragmatic attitude of the "materialist society." For example, various prejudices have changed recently. The abhorrence of homosexuality is waning, because well-educated people realize that certain sexual behavior is genetically predetermined. The homosexuality issue is an active religious topic; it has been very divisive in the Anglican-Episcopalian Churches. Also, the sin of adultery is no longer considered a serious transgression. In those religions where it is still a major sin, there are ways of sidestepping the problem, such as "short term" marriages practiced in some Islamic societies. Religious leaders can cope with these problems by realizing that absolute truths are no longer acceptable to the population as a whole.

Education

In the past, religious dogma was supported throughout the world by both education systems and governments. Many governments were based on religious law, although there was often conflict with secular rule. Religious education was the primary path of learning. Religious schools still dominate in some cultures, especially in areas of the Muslim world, but most people realize that this form of education is generally too rigid. Eventually, about two hundred years ago, most governments in the advanced nations of the world became secular and much more democratic. Concurrently, education became secular, resulting in major advances in civilization. These changes in education and government occurred partly because of the moral decline of religious leaders, and partly because of the slow adaptation of religions to social and scientific changes. The long term effect on mankind of secular education and the separation of church and state has been positive. The rapid increase in scientific knowledge since secularization has resulted in an enormous improvement in the welfare of mankind, for example man's life span and standard of living.

Modern secular education is the enemy of religious fundamentalists in all lands. The former, short-lived Taliban government of Afghanistan strongly resisted secular education, and indeed any education for females. The present (2006) Taliban resistance movement there has viciously destroyed schools and assassinated teachers. In the USA, fundamentalists also resist forms of education that conflict with their religious dogma. For example, they want the teaching of the theory of evolution to be modified by creation "theory," hiding behind an "intelligent design" concept.

An essential element for reform within religions, and understanding among religions, is the universal liberal education of all citizens. It is of utmost importance in the struggle against fanaticism. Young children should be taught tolerance and respect for other religions and cultures. Classes in comparative religion and world culture could be mandatory in every school curriculum. Every day there are hate crimes and religious massacres around the world. Intolerance and hate are learned. Generations have been taught from early childhood by their parents and peers to hate various religious and ethnic groups. Throughout history, humans have oppressed and killed their fellows in the name of religious or ethnic "superiority" or "inferiority." If intolerance and hate can be taught, then tolerance and love can also be taught. In a child's formative years, the education system should teach the history and lore of different religious beliefs, in order to achieve understanding and tolerance of different faiths. Such teaching does not conflict with separation of church and state. Also, the schools should teach children about the world's different ethnic groups, their traditions and cultures. Such a program would foster tolerance, if not love, of different religions, cultures, and ethnic values.

Democracy

To retain their influence in the world, religious leaders would be advised to develop a more democratic governance. Although democratization is difficult, since religion is based on dogmatic codes and beliefs, some progress in adaptation and democratization has already occurred. Especially in the Christian faiths, diversification and development of new religious concepts of faith and governance have evolved. This is perhaps why Christianity is the dominant religion of the world, in spite of its many failings and transgressions. One of the most important revolutions in Christian thought and democratization was the Protestant Reformation. It was a reaction of the people—through strong religious leaders such as Luther and Calvin—to certain abuses and practices of the existing Roman Catholic Church. In religions, there is always a struggle between retaining the traditional dogma and developing new ideas. Even within the lifetime of major religious leaders, such as Muhammad, perceptions of their faith changed. Concepts of God have evolved with time; for example, the original vengeful, tribal Jehovah of Judaism has been replaced by a more benevolent, loving God. Consequently, it is clear that religions have adapted, and, in some cases, become more democratic, to represent the will of the people and the common good. A good example of early democratization occurred in the Anglican Church of England, where bishops and deans were elected by the parishioners.

The Roman Catholic Church and the Episcopal Church (USA) illustrate opposite modern extremes of democracy in Christian faiths. The Catholic Pope is elected by the College of Cardinals upon the death of the previous Pope. Since the Cardinals are appointed by the Popes, there is considerable likelihood of favoritism. In the past, especially in the days of the Medici Popes of the sixteenth century (see Ch. 5.5), many nonecclesiastical cardinals were appointed by the Popes, and the papacy was effectively bought and sold. As a result of the strict hierarchal governance of the Catholic Church, reforms have been very slow. Catholic laity would probably prefer a more democratic Church. If there were a vote of all Catholics regarding methods of birth control, priestly celibacy and female ordination, undoubtedly the Pope's positions in these areas would be overturned.

In contrast, the Episcopal Church of the USA, which is the American version of the worldwide Anglican Church, follows a democratic form of religious governance. As a result, it is among the most liberal and tolerant of churches. Clergy do not have to be celibate. For many years, women have been ordained as priests (but not in all dioceses). In 2003, a homosexual bishop, Gene Robinson, was consecrated in New Hampshire. In 2006, Katharine Jefferts Schori was elected as the first female head of the Church. These two events have caused extreme angst within the more traditional members, so that congregations and even dioceses have threatened to break away from the main Church.

Such strife is inevitable, as fundamentalist forces strive to retain some outdated and misguided beliefs, based on ancient dogma. There will always be conflict in the unending process of human development. This conflict will lead to a more moral, more loving, and more tolerant religious community.

Spirituality

The fanatic belief in the superiority of a particular version of religion and the striving for power caused calamitous struggles within and between religions. Christianity suffered from the separation of the Roman Catholic Church from the Eastern Orthodox Church, the persecution of the Cathars and Anabaptists, and the disastrous Thirty Years War—a culmination of the Reformation. Conflicts within eastern religions were less intense than in the West. The creation of the Buddhist movement from Hinduism, and the schism in Buddhism between the Lesser and Greater Paths to Salvation, were relatively peaceful, perhaps because of their more spiritual attitudes. Wars between major religions have also been disastrous, for example, the Crusades. The present "war on terrorism" is really just an extension of the fourteen hundred-year struggle between Christianity and Islam. Such struggles do not inspire faith in the redemptive qualities of religion. The basic reason for these conflicts is the fanatic desire for power. A compensating influence is spirituality. A person who believes that all of mankind is infused with the spirit of God, that God exists in every human, rarely has the audacity to claim that his God or spiritual wisdom is superior to that of others.

It seems that liberal education, democratization, renewed spirituality and general reform of religions can prevent or at least reduce fanaticism and religious conflicts. Recently, the relative peace and prosperity within Europe and North America, in the environment of tolerant reformed churches, can be contrasted with the strife and misery of those areas controlled by the fundamentalist Wahhabi and other sects of Islam in the Middle East and Africa.

Communication

Another important area for improvement of religions is communication. The best religious minds can be assembled, in a democratic way, to discuss, reassess and reorganize religious doctrine and administration. The process should be done within each religion and among religions.

Some progress has been made in this direction by Ecumenical Councils within Catholic, Protestant and Anglican organizations. Several national and international mergers of churches have occurred in the Protestant and Anglican faiths. Significant progress has also been achieved toward worldwide religious ecumenism by the World Council of Churches, a Christian union of many Orthodox and Protestant Churches, but not including the Roman Catholic Church. This Council has organized meetings among as many as ten world faiths, to promote cooperation among the world's religious bodies. Religious problems have been discussed, but solutions are elusive. Proselytizing is still actively practiced, primarily by Christian churches. It hinders the dialogue between Roman Catholic and Eastern Orthodox Churches. Islam objects strongly to this practice. Regarding this issue, the recent election of Pope Benedict XVI indicates that further progress is unlikely in the near future. In his book *Truth and Tolerance: Christian Belief and World Religions* (Joseph Ratzinger, Ignatius Press, 2004), he endorses St. Peter's conviction, as related in Acts 4:12, that Jesus is the only savior: "There is no salvation through anyone else, nor is there any other name under heaven given to the human race by which we are to be saved." This is a very divisive and inflammatory statement. Modern religious thought, for example in reformed sects, can overcome this dogmatic adherence to scripture. If every religion considered that their holy texts were the only and final words of God, then reconciliation would be hopeless. Many religious leaders realize that the stories in various holy scriptures are allegories and fables, rather than fact. Taking the word of scripture literally leads to fanatic viewpoints, like the death penalty for apostasy. Such perversions of divine inspiration can be overturned by the mainstream of sensible religious leaders and informed laymen, to achieve a consensus of reasonable doctrines among the world's religions.

Religion can contribute once again to the betterment of mankind, by reforming dogma, discarding fanaticism, and resisting the desire for power. These goals can be accomplished by using the powerful tools of education, democratization and communication. Religion can utilize the strength of its majority of moderates to renew its role as a spiritual and moral leader. Spirituality can triumph over fanaticism.

CONCLUSIONS

The righteous of all nations are worthy of immortality.
—Jewish Talmud

Creativity requires the courage to let go of certainties.
—Erich Fromm

Religions were created by humans from ancient myths, to worship the God or gods that created the universe. The faith and spirituality implicit in religions (Chs. 1 and 2) should have ennobled humans. Instead, throughout history, religion has been plagued by intolerance, persecutions, and wars, that have negated the benevolence (Ch. 10) contained in all religious doctrine. The problems besetting religion arose from three basic flaws of human behavior: fanaticism, lust for power, and rigid dogmatism (Chs. 3, 5, and 6). These weaknesses in humans cannot be eliminated, but their influence in religion can be mitigated by a renewal of religious spirituality, which is basically incompatible with those flaws. Of equal importance for the reform of religions are universal education, improved communication within and among religions, and democratization of religious governance.

Religion was once considered essential to create order in society, and to provide a moral code for human behavior. Is it still useful or necessary? Can the influence of fundamentalist, uncompromising religious ideas be stopped, or at least marginalized? Can basic human flaws—such as greed, vanity, pride, and, above all, the striving for individual and group power—be overcome within religious sects? The principles and

175

moral codes of most religions inspire believers to practice humility rather than arrogance, understanding rather than intolerance, meekness rather than power, charity rather than greed, and love rather than hate. Unfortunately, the very teachers, officials and leaders of many religions throughout history have violated the laws and codes of their own religions. The doctrines and philosophies of religions promote a just and peaceful society, but humans administer religions, and often corrupt them to further their personal, tribal and ethnic ambitions.

History could have been changed if religious leaders had been less interested in dogma and power, and more devoted to practicing their own moral codes. Consider the example of the Cathars, a sect of the Roman Catholic Church that adopted a somewhat different, dualist view of God during the Middle Ages (Ch. 5). The Pope and his advisors decided that this sect was becoming too powerful, and therefore had to be eliminated. The ensuing massacre of the Cathars was an immoral result of the Church seeking ultimate power over all the peoples of Europe. The persecution of the Cathars, and of many other groups who defied the power of the Church, was to continue for many centuries, culminating in the infamous "Inquisition." A more insightful and less dogmatic, power-seeking and fanatic church would have attempted to reconcile the differences in ideologies, which, after all, were not so great, seen from the modern perspective. For example, the Anabaptists simply did not believe that baptism was necessary for infants. Surely, some compromise was feasible. If the laity and religious leaders had received a more liberal and less dogmatic education in their early lives, if the clergy in the opposing faiths had communicated better and discussed their differences, and if the governance of the religious factions had been more democratic, these disasters could have been avoided.

In contrast to these Christian failings, an outstanding example of cooperation among different faiths was the coexistence of Confucianism, Taoism, and Buddhism in China for many centuries. As the Chinese said, "The three teachings flow into one." The purpose of those three faiths, to improve the physical and spiritual welfare of the Chinese people, was clearly more important to their leaders than the achievement of supreme power. Their example could be emulated by modern religious leaders.

The three demons of religion, namely fanaticism, lust for power, and inflexibility, can be rolled into one flaw: the fanatic lust for power, based on inflexible adherence to outdated and misguided dogma. Many cruel injustices and deaths could have been avoided if religious leaders had respected women (Ch.8), revered sexuality (Ch. 7), and refrained from committing the sins (Ch. 9) that they preached against. Humankind would have been much more peaceful if religious leaders had not exerted their power to subjugate aboriginal peoples, and to force other sects and nations to submit to their religious views.

Is there hope for religion in the future? Yes, if religious leaders throw off the yokes of dogmatism and intolerance, their fanatic devotion to one path to salvation, and their desire to force their frail version of spirituality on others. Progress can be achieved by a universal striving for and acceptance of democratic reforms within religion. Women must be given completely equal rights in all religions. Since this equality has not yet been achieved in many secular societies, which have less rigid governance than religions, the goal of female equality within religion will remain elusive for some time. A considerable amount of freedom and tolerance has been achieved in the secular world through democratic government by all the people. A similar transformation can occur in religious organizations. Some progress has been made in the democratization of religions.

Equally important for the future of religion is the development of more effective communication within each religion, and among the many religions of the world. The meetings of various worldwide ecumenical councils of churches (Ch. 11) have produced encouraging results. However, religious leaders will have to discard their conviction that their forms of salvation and religious ideals are the only ones dictated by God. Then, a general consensus concerning the nature of God, and the doctrines appropriate for human morals and behavior will be achievable.

Ultimately, the reform of religion requires the enlightenment of the mind of man, achievable through the universal, liberal education of all people, including instruction in tolerance for all religions and cultures of the world. The effectiveness of universal secular education is profound and undeniable.

A return to the spiritual base of religion will aid in combating fanaticism, rigid dogmatism and the thirst for power. Organized religion has unfortunately all but discarded spirituality in favor of power and influence. The basis of spirituality is the existence of the divine in all humans. A person who believes that principle is tolerant of other faiths, and has no wish to impose his will on others.

EPILOGUE

I weep for all those who were persecuted and killed in the name of religion.

I forgive all those who persecuted and killed in the name of religion.

I pray that the persecution and killing will cease.

GENERAL REFERENCES

The Catholic Encyclopedia (http://www.newadvent.org/cathen/index.html)

Encyclopedia Britannica, various editions

The Free Encyclopedia (Wikipedia.org)

Religious Tolerance (http://www.religioustolerance.org/)

Questia (www.questia.com)

World Christian Encyclopedia: A comparative survey of churches and religions in the Modern World, Eds. David B. Barrett, George T. Kurian, Todd M. Johnson, Oxford University Press, 2001

* * *

The Age of Faith: A History of Medieval Civilization—Christian, Islamic, and Judaic—from Constantine to Dante: A.D. 325-1300, Will Durant, Simon and Schuster, New York, 1950

Buddhism: A Way of Life and Thought, Nancy Wilson Ross, Vintage Books USA, 1981

The Christians, Bamber Gascoigne, Jonathan Cape Press, London, 1986

The End of Faith: Religion, Terror, and the Future of Reason. Sam Harris, W. W. Norton & Company, New York, 2004

Farewell to God: My Reasons for Rejecting the Christian Faith, Charles Templeton, McClelland & Stewart 1999

The Foundations of Buddhism, Rupert Gethin, Oxford University Press, 1998

The God Delusion, Richard Dawkins, Bantam Press, 2006

Guns, Germs and Steel: The Fates of Human Societies, Jared Diamond, W. W. Norton, 2005

A History of God, the 4000 Year Quest of Judaism, Christianity and Islam, Karen Armstrong, Alfred A. Knopf, New York, 1994

Hinduism, Vasudha Narayanan, Oxford University Press, Oxford, 2004

Islam in America, Jane I. Smith, Columbia University Press, New York, 1999

Islam: Religion, History and Civilization, Seyyed Hossein Nasr, Harper San Francisco, New York, 2003

Man's Religions, John B. Noss, Macmillan Publishing Co., New York, 1974

The March of Folly: From Troy to Vietnam, Barbara W. Tuchman, Ballantine Books, New York, 1985

The Pagan Christ: Recovering the Lost Light, Tom Harpur, Walker and Co., New York, 2005

The Social Teaching of the Christian Churches, (Translation of Die Soziallehren der christlichen Kirchen und Gruppen, 1912), Ernst Troeltsch, Harper Press, 1960

CHAPTER BIBLIOGRAPHY

CHAPTER 1

Ch 1.1
The Hero with a Thousand Faces, Joseph Campbell, Princeton University Press, Princeton, 1972

The Inner Reaches of Outer Space: Metaphor as Myth and as Religion, Joseph Campbell, New World Library, Novato, Calif., 1986

The Power of Myth, Joseph Campbell, with Bill Moyers, Anchor Books, New York, 1991

Gospel Truth: The New Image of Jesus Emerging from Science and History, and Why It Matters Russell Shorto Riverhead Books, New York, 1997

Ch 1.2
The Age of Faith: A History of Medieval Civilization—Christian, Islamic, and Judaic—from Constantine to Dante: A.D. 325-1300 Will Durant Simon and Schuster, New York, 1950

CHAPTER 2

Ch 2.1
Gods of the Earth: *The Quest for the Mother Goddess and the Sacred King*, Michael Jordan, Bantam Press, 1992

Ch 2.2

Life After Death: A History of the Afterlife in the Religions of the West, Alan F. Segal, Doubleday, New York, 2004.

Life After Death: A Study of the Afterlife in World Religions, Farnaz Ma'Sumian, Oneworld Publishers, Oxford, 1995

Life After Death, Tom Harpur, McClelland and Stewart, Toronto, 1991.

Die Syro-Aramäische Lesart des Koran (The Syro-Aramaic Reading of the Koran), Christoph Luxenberg, Berlin: Verlag Hans Schiler, 2004.

What the Koran Really Says, Ed. Ibn Warraq, Prometheus Books, 2002

Ch 2.3

Hear Then the Parable: A Commentary on the Parables of Jesus, Bernard Brandon Scott, Fortress Press, Minneapolis, 1990.

Buddhism; A Way of Life and Thought, Nancy Wilson Ross, Vintage Books USA, 1981

The Three Pillars of Zen, Roshi Philip Kapleau, Knopf Publishing Group, New York, 1980

Taking the Path of Zen, Robert Aitken, North Point Press, San Francisco, 1984

The Miracle of Mindfulness, Thich Nhat Hahn, Beacon Press, 1987

Ch 2.4

Holy Blood, Holy Grail, Michael Baigent, Richard Leigh and Henry Lincoln, Dell, 1983

The Da Vinci Code, Dan Brown, Doubleday, New York, 2003

The Pagan Christ: Recovering the Lost Light, Tom Harpur, Walker and Co., New York, 2005

The Gospel of Mary of Magdala: Jesus and the First Woman Apostle, Karen L. King, Polebridge Press, Santa Rosa, CA, 2003

Ch 2.5
"Sufism," Wikipedia.org

Masnavi Mawlana Rumi, Jalal al-Din Rumi, Kazi Publications Inc., 1996

Ch 2.6
The Pagan Christ: Recovering the Lost Light, Tom Harpur, Walker and Co., New York, 2005

A Rebirth for Christianity, Alvin Boyd Kuhn, Quest Books, 2005

CHAPTER 3

Ch 3.2
Abraham, Bruce Feiler, Williams Morrow Publishing, New York, 2002

Ch 3.3
The Messianic Legacy Michael Baigent Richard Leigh and Henry Lincoln, Arrow Books, 1996

Why the Jews? The Reason for Antisemitism, Dennis Prager and Joseph Telushkin, a Touchstone Book, Simon and Schuster, New York, 1983

Faith after the Holocaust, Eliezer Berkovits, Ktav Pub Inc.,1977

Ch 3.4
The Book of Ser Marco Polo, the Venetian, translated by Henry Yule, London, 1875

Ch 3.5

"How the Holy Warriors Learned to Hate," Waleed Ziad, New York Times newspaper, June 18, 2004

Ch 3.6

Palestinian Jewish settlers quotes: http://www.telrumeidaproject. org/settler_quotes.html

"Cave of the Patriarchs Massacre," Wikipedia.org

"Heil Druckman!" by Michael A. Hoffman, RevisionistHistory. org

CHAPTER 4

Ch 4.1

The Social Teaching of the Christian Churches, (Translation of *Die Soziallehren der christlichen Kirchen und Gruppen*, 1912), Ernst Troeltsch, Harper Press, 1960

Ch 4.2

"Children of God," Wikipedia.org

Science and Health with Key to the Scriptures., Mary Baker Eddy, publisher: Trustees of Eddy, Boston,1934 (also available online)

Dianetics: The Modern Science of Mental Health, L. Ron Hubbard, Hermitage House, 1950

"Seven brides for one brother: Plural marriage is rife in the western United States," Suzan Mazur, Financial Times, Oct.28, 2000

Ch 4.3

Messengers of Deception: UFO Contacts and Cults, Jacques Vallee, Ronin Publishers, 1979

The Gods Have Landed: New Religions from Other Worlds, James R. Lewis, Ed., State University of New York Press, Albany, NY, 1995

Hearing the Voices of Jonestown, M. McCormick Maaga and Catherine Wessinger, Syracuse University Press, Syracuse, NY, 1998

Seductive Poison: A Jonestown Survivor's Story of Life and Death in the Peoples Temple, Deborah Layton Blakey, Doubleday,1998

Raven: The untold story of Reverend Jim Jones and his people, Tim Reiterman & John Jacobs, E.P. Dutton, 1982.

Cults in America: Programmed for Paradise, Willa Appel, Holt Rinehart & Winston, Fort Worth, Texas,1983

Cult Controversies: The Societal Response to the New Religious Movements, J A Beckford, Tavistock, London,1985

Ch 4.4
Battle for the Mind: A Physiology of Conversion and Brain-Washing, William Sargant, Doubleday, New York, 1957

Snapping: America's Epidemic of Sudden Personality Change, Flo Conway and Jim Siegelman, Stillpoint Press, 1995

CHAPTER 5

Ch 5.1
On Aggression, Konrad Lorenz, Harcourt, Brace and Co, New York, 1966

Ch 5.2
Collapse: How Societies Choose to Fail or Succeed, Jared Diamond, Viking Press, New York, 2005

Rivers of Blood, Rivers of Gold. Europe's Conquest of Indigenous Peoples, Mark Cocker, New York, 1998.

Guns, Germs and Steel: The Fates of Human Societies, Jared Diamond, W. W. Norton, 2005

A Short Account of the Destruction of the Indies, Father Bartolome de Las Casas, Penguin Classics, 1992

Yucatan Before and After the Conquest, Friar Diego de Landa, Produccion Editorial Dante, Merida, Mexico, 1990

Fingerprints of the Gods, Graham Hancock, Three Rivers Press, 1996

Mysteries of the Mexican Pyramids, Peter Tompkins, Thames and Hudson, London, 1987

Wild Majesty: Encounters with Caribs from Columbus to the Present Day, P. Hulme and N. Whitehead, Oxford, 1992

Ch 5.3
The Inquisitor's Manual of Bernard Gui, early 14th century, translated in J. H. Robinson, *Readings in European History*, Boston: Ginn, 1905

The Crusades: A Documentary History, James Brundage, Marquette University Press, Milwaukee, 1962, from his translation of the *Chronica Regiae Coloniensis Continuatio prima*

Ch 5.4
"Canadian residential school system", Wikipedia.org.

"Canadian Royal Commission Report on Aboriginal Peoples," Library of Parliament, 1996

Shingwauk's vision: A history of Canadian residential schools, J. R. Miller, University of Toronto Press, 1996

Ch 5.5
The March of Folly: From Troy to Vietnam, Barbara W. Tuchman, Ballantine Books, New York,1985

CHAPTER 6

Ch 6.1
Farewell to God: My Reasons for Rejecting the Christian Faith, Charles Templeton, McClelland & Stewart, 1999

De Trinitate, St. Augustine

Ch 6.3
Papal Sin: Structures of Deceit, Garry Wills, Doubleday, New York, 2000.

Casti Connubii (On Christian Marriage), 55, Encyclical, Pope Pius XI, 1930

Humanae Vitae, Encyclical, Pope Paul VI, 1968.

The New Testament and Homosexuality, Robin Scroggs Augsburg Fortress Publishers, 1983

Ch 6.4
Islam in America, Jane I. Smith, Columbia University Press, New York, 1999

CHAPTER 7

A History of God, the 4000 Year Quest of Judaism, Christianity and Islam, Karen Armstrong, Alfred A. Knopf, New York, 1994

Ch 7.1
Nine Parts of Desire: The Hidden World of Islamic Women, Geraldine Brooks, Doubleday, 1994

Ch 7.2
Sacrament of Sexuality, Morton & Barbara Kelsey, Element Books, Rockport, MA 1991

The Good of Marriage, St. Augustine of Hippo, Letters

Ch 7.3
Mandatory Celibacy in the Catholic Church—A Handbook for the Laity, Michele Prince, New Paradigm Books, Pasadena, CA, 1992;

Celibacy in the Early Church, Stefan Heid, Ignatius Press, San Francisco, CA, 1997

The Body and Society—Men, Women and Sexual Renunciation in Early Christianity, Peter Brown, Columbia University Press, New York, NY, 1988

Papal Sin: Structures of Deceit, Garry Wills, Doubleday, New York, 2000

"Celibacy," in Wikipedia.org

"A Brief History of Celibacy in the Catholic Church," FutureChurch.org

Ch 7.4
"The Nature and Scope of the Problem of Sexual Abuse of Minors by Catholic Priests and Deacons in the United States," A Research Study Conducted by the John Jay College of Criminal Justice, 2004

Papal Sin: Structures of Deceit, Garry Wills, Doubleday, New York, 2000.

"Rudolf Kos and the Catholic diocese of Dallas," Dallas Morning News, July 25, 1997

Ch 7.5
United Nations Children's Fund (UNICEF) report, "Early Marriage: Child Spouses," 2001

"Aisha," Wikipedia.org

Ch 7.6
The Kama Sutra of Vatsyayana, Sir Richard Burton, translator (1883)—Currently available as *The Illustrated Kama Sutra: Ananga-Ranga and Perfumed Garden—The Classic Eastern Love Texts*, Sir Richard F. Burton (Translator), F. F. Arbuthnot (Translator), Park Street Press; New Ed Edition,1991

CHAPTER 8

Ch 8.1
Papal Sin: Structures of Deceit, Garry Wills, Doubleday, New York, 2000

Gospel of Mary of Magdala: Jesus and the First Woman Apostle, Karen L. King, Polebridge Press, Santa Rosa, CA, 2003

Women and Men in the Early Church: The Full Views of St. John Chrysostom, David Ford, St Tikhons Seminary Press,1996

Ch 8.2
Marriage, a History: From Obedience to Intimacy, or How Love Conquered Marriage, Stephanie Coontz, Viking Press, New York, 2005

Islam in America, Jane I. Smith, Columbia University Press, New York,1999

Islam: Religion, History and Civilization, Seyyed Hossein Nasr, Harper, San Francisco, New York, 2003

"International Woman Suffrage Timeline," http://womenshistory.about.com

Ch 8.4
Itqaan Fee Ulum Al-Quran, Vol. 2, Jalaluddin Al-Suyuti, Al-Azhareyyah Press, Cairo, Egypt

Ch 8.5
"Bride Burning": wikipedia.org

"Plight of Widows in India," Jyotsna Kamat, www.kamat.com/kalranga/women/widows/

Ch 8.6
"Sentenced to Be Raped," Nicholas Kristof, New York Times, Sept. 29, 2004

CHAPTER 9

Ch 9.1
Satanic Verses: A Novel, Salman Rushdie, Picador USA, 2000

Ch 9.2
A History of God, the 4000 Year Quest of Judaism, Christianity and Islam, Karen Armstrong, Alfred A. Knopf, New York, 1994

CHAPTER 11

Truth and Tolerance: Christian Belief and World Religions, Joseph Ratzinger, Ignatius Press, 2004

Author's Cover Bio

Max Swanson was born in 1931 in Michigan, USA, and was raised in Vancouver, Canada, where he received a PhD in metal physics from the University of British Columbia. He worked as a research scientist for Atomic Energy of Canada from 1960 to 1986, and was a professor of physics at the University of North Carolina, Chapel Hill from 1986 to 1993. He has published more than 150 scientific papers. He lives in Kelowna, Canada, in the summer and near Sarasota, USA, in winter. He is married with four children and eleven grandchildren.

Book Summary

Religions were created by humans from ancient myths. The spirituality, faith, and morality that are implicit in religions should have ennobled humans. Instead, throughout history, religion has been plagued by intolerance, persecutions, and wars that negated the benevolence contained in all religious doctrine. The problems besetting religion arise from fanaticism, lust for power, and dogmatism. These aspects of religion, as well as spirituality and the role of women, are discussed. The means for reforming religion are universal liberal education, religious democratization, improved communication among religions, and a renewal of spirituality.

INDEX

Printed in the United Kingdom
by Lightning Source UK Ltd.
134418UK00001B/34/A

9 781425 756307